Betting in the Twenty-First Century

Challenges and opportunities for the modern punter

Ricky Taylor

First published, 2020

ISBN: 9798650529262

To Jess

CONTENTS

ABOUT THE AUTHOR

Ricky Taylor, a horse racing fan and punter since the age of seven, has spent many years researching betting systems and strategies. He previously authored the books *Pace Wins The Race* and *Profitable Betting Systems for Horseracing*. You can read his latest research and analysis at profitablebetting.co.uk.

INTRODUCTION

Horse racing maybe one of the oldest of all sports, and in its essentials it would appear to have undergone virtually no change over the centuries – it is still about thoroughbreds racing across a large field – but in so many other ways it is constantly evolving and the pace of change has accelerated considerably in the twenty-first century. The changes over the last twenty years have been profound and have radically altered the betting environment for the punter. These changes though have largely gone unnoticed or have been passively accepted by most of the betting public. However those that have noticed and adapted to the changes have been able to reap the rewards at the expense of the rest.

The reactionaries might argue that while the advent of betting exchanges, such as Betfair in June 2000, has produced a significant shift in the betting industry the actual sport of horse racing itself is still basically the same. Punters that accept this view will still think that they can evaluate races in the same way that they always have, and that the winner finding methods of yesterday year will still work today. The reality is that the volume of digital information available, the sophistication of others to generate meaningful statistics and generate new insights from the data means that the traditionalists are simply food for those that have embraced the twenty-first century.

The idea that horse racing is fixed in aspic defies the facts. The racehorse itself is improving thanks to better breeding and because of advances in veterinary science and training methods. Jockey's riding styles have also improved and these factors in combination now mean that today's thoroughbreds are fitter and faster than their predecessors of only a few years ago. The modern punter needs to be alive to these developments.

A good example is sire analysis. Few punters bother to look at the breeding of a horse because they consider it irrelevant but in some kinds of races, such as sprint races, the sire of the horse is now exerting more of an influence on the result of a race because these races are getting quicker and require horses with more speed. Research shows that since the 1850s turf flat races over six furlongs or less have been getting steadily quicker, but particularly in the last twenty years. To most punters this fact may not mean much but it actually means that some types of races, particularly sprints, are placing more emphasis on speed and so horses bred from sires that are more likely to pass on speed genes to their offspring have a bigger advantage in those kinds of races than they once did.

Today's trainers are also able to get their horses fitter than their predecessors because they have adapted new techniques and many have all-weather gallops. Any dinosaurs among the training ranks are soon made extinct because it is now far harder to win a race at any level unless it is super fit. The early pioneers of these training methods reaped rich rewards, as did the punters that latched onto them early-on. The big edge of following runners from Martin Pipe's stable went pretty quickly but if you keep yourself up-to-date good trainer analysis still pays off and it still helps to identify good up-and-coming trainers, and trainers that are better than the rest at getting a horse race fit after a lay-off.

One of the biggest changes effecting the punter is one that is largely ignored because at first it seems irrelevant to picking winners. It is the move over the centuries from horse racing being a sporting pursuit run by amateur enthusiasts to being a major industry run by business people for commercial advantage. A related development has been changes in the way the government has funded horse racing. Racing is now funded by a levy on bookmakers profits rather than on a levy on punters bets. These fairly recent developments have completely transformed the racing programme and what punters can bet on, and this requires punters to change their betting strategies.

The consequence of these changes for the punter is that they now have thousands more races to bet on than they did in the past because more racing means more turnover for bookmakers, more potential profits, and more income for the racing industry. It also means that the race programme is now dominated more than ever by handicaps because handicap races, particularly ones with large field sizes, generate more profits for bookmakers because most punters basically find it harder to pick a winner in these sorts of races than in stakes races. The modern backer though can turn this to his or her advantage because handicaps require more skill and can give a bit of an edge to those that have a better than average form analysis behind them. However, I still hear people tell that old adage about 'never bet in a handicap'. If you follow that advice you would struggle these days to find much to bet on, and certainly not enough opportunities to consistently make your racing pay.

Handicaps also give the unwary punter the illusion of value because the odds on a favourite in a large field handicap are almost always going to be higher than for a favourite in a stakes race. This doesn't mean that the favourite in a handicap is better value than the short priced favourite in a stakes race. It all depends on the true odds of the horse winning and the odds of reward. This is a lesson that too many in the game have still failed to learn, but this is to the advantage of the modern twenty-first century punter. Those that understand the concept of value are the ones that will turn in a long-term profit.

There have certainly been a lot of changes to horse racing and horse race betting since the turn of the century. The most obvious is the widespread use of the internet and the amount of information that is now available to the punter in the digital age. This is a double edged sword for the modern backer. The availability of information, such as statistics, video form, expert advice, and research databases make it much easier to do more sophisticated form analysis than ever before. However, the downside is that the availability of information makes it easy for anyone to access the same information, and the value of that information therefore falls.

In theory this should make it much harder to make a profit from backing horses because all the available information will be incorporated into the horses odds. Consequently there is less chance of a punter finding an angle that will give them an edge over other punters because everyone else has access to the same information. There is some element of truth to this because I remember the days when you could gain a huge advantage as a punter if you went racing regularly because so few races were screened on television, and you could spot something in a race than no one else had noticed. Those days are gone with free video form readily available. However, the twenty-first century punter realises that the sheer volume of information now available can also make people blind. Simply having vast amounts of information available to you will not in itself give you better insight.

The ability to process all the information available now is beyond human capabilities. Every bit of information is also not of equal value. Much of it will be garbage. This is what data scientists call a signal and noise problem because the data is making a lot of noise but it is hard to find the signal within it to help us make better (and profitable) decisions. The successful modern backer knows that he or she is better off investing in tools or expert research that help to weed through all the data to find the really important information, and to weight it appropriately. This might mean acquiring new analytical or IT skills, and/or investing in services that can do this for them.

In this book I try to bring together a range of research and analysis that I have conducted into flat and jump racing with the intention that it will give you an edge in your betting. I also hope to provide you with advice about how you can stay ahead of other punters in the twenty-first century.

I start in Chapter One with the racehorse. You would think that the one constant in horse racing would be the racehorse but as I explained earlier the latest scientific research shows that racehorses are actually getting faster. However, while this might be a general trend, my own in-depth analysis shows that horses themselves actually don't like change in terms of changes in race distance, going or class level. We do though know more about the preferences of horses by being able to analyse the form book in more depth as a result of computer form databases, and I look at ways in which you can spot horses that might improve when getting their ideal conditions.

This century punters also have a bit more raw data to play with, and in Chapter One I also look at the data on horses that have had wind operations now that this information has to be declared by trainers and printed in racecards. I also look at sectional times as these are now slowly being made available, although only for some racecourses.

In Chapter Two I contend that in the twenty-first century there has also been a definite improvement in jockeyship, and I report on the latest scientific evidence that demonstrates that jockey's today are so much fitter and more professional in comparison to the jockeys of just a few decades ago. However, the problem for the punter in the modern era is that the improvements in jockeyship have narrowed the difference between the best and the worst jockeys. In the 1980s and even in the 1990s you could quickly work out which jockeys couldn't even ride a bike. These days it is harder to spot the jockey that can improve a horse or is least likely to unseat. The modern backer therefore needs to use more sophisticated statistics in order to identify subtle differences in jockey ability, and in this Chapter I set out a couple of methods for doing exactly that.

Chapter Three concerns the owner, breeder and the trainer. In my view the twenty-first century has made it more important than ever before to side with the horse that has the right connections. My rationale is that those owners that are at the top of the tree, such as Sheikh Mohammed and Coolmore, have the financial power to provide the best training facilities and utilise the latest advances in science and technology to give them an edge. This is more true today than in the past because the use of science and technology in horse racing has rapidly accelerated this century. For the punter this means that it pays more to identify horses with the best connections in terms of owner and trainer, and to use the data properly to understand when the horses connections are at the top of their game.

Chapter Four discusses how the relationship between the punter and the bookmaker has changed radically this century following the advent of betting exchanges. As a result of this development the modern punter is now both a backer and a layer. The modern punter needs to be able to exploit the opportunities that this new world creates. I discuss elsewhere in this book the strategies that can be deployed to do this but in this Chapter I detail some of the psychological challenges that this brave new world has created, such as the roller-coaster of emotions that betting in-play can evoke. I also provide some stories of professional modern backers, such as Bill Benter and Alan Woods, who really embraced technology and the use of modern statistics to earn fantastic profits from their betting.

Chapter Five concerns the racing tipster. The tipster has certainly been one of the few constants over the decades, and tipsters have been around since racing began. Most are useless but some aren't and one of the things that has changed this century is that there is now more information available to be able to differentiate between those tipsters who genuinely know something about the game and those that don't. In this Chapter I detail some of my research on newspaper naps and other publicly available ratings, including some research that I did on the Racing Post Pricewise service.

Chapter Six focuses on the racecourse. The twenty-first century has seen a number of changes to the number and nature of British racecourses. At present we have 59 racecourses operating in Great Britain. A number of tracks are under threat of closure or mothballed, For a number of years racecourses have struggled to compete for the leisure pound, especially in more remote rural locations. The almost endless rise in house prices has also made the land on which they are situated more and more valuable. These economic pressures look likely to continue. It remains to be seen whether this will lead to more racecourse closures in the twenty-first century but in the twentieth century racing lost scores of racecourses to the developers.

The economic pressures on racecourses might see more of a move towards all-weather racing, and a racing programme based around our major tracks. The modern punter might be better off studying the biases at these tracks and in Chapter Six I offer some analysis and systems that might help.

In the twenty-first century the betting market is no longer the betting ring at a racecourse. It lives in the digital cloud, with people trading with each other on the outcome of races on the exchanges. In Chapter Seven I discuss whether the betting market can be a guide to winners and whether you can consistently beat the odds by focussing on value selections. To this end I describe how you can create your own 'tissue' prices, and use the famous Kelly staking plan to maximise your stakes on those bets that give you the biggest edge.

In Chapter Eight I discuss how you can now have your betting systems automated and your bets made automatically by computer bots. This would have been the stuff of fantasy in the 1980s and 1990s but is now a reality in the 2000's. However, you need to have good strategies in the first place before you think about betting automatically. A losing strategy will always be a losing strategy and automation won't help. In fact it might just help you to lose your money quicker. In this Chapter I therefore offer several systems that might help you.

In Chapter Nine I discuss the new tools of the trade for the modern backer, such as form databases; statistical analysis software; the Betfair API; and how you can use programming languages such as SQL, Perl and R to develop highly sophisticated automated systems. This chapter may not be for everyone but it might provide a few pointers for those that want to move on to the next level in their betting and want to fully embrace the twenty-first century approach to betting.

I continue the theme of betting systems in Chapter 10 by offering a few pointers on how to develop your own systems and strategies. The widespread availability of online form databases and software have made it easier to research your own systems. However, there are some pitfalls that you need to avoid when researching your own systems and in this Chapter I try to steer you in the right direction (I hope!).

Horse racing has changed a great deal since the turn of the century. The sport and the betting industry around it will continue to evolve. Wider developments such as the digital revolution have also completely changed the landscape of information that is available to the punter and have given them the ability to bet online in many different ways. These developments present challenges to the punter, but they also provide profitable opportunities to the backer who adapts best to these changes.

2 THE RACEHORSE

You would think that the performance of the racehorse has been one of the few constants in horse racing. After all a horse is a horse. However, the latest scientific research has shown that racehorses are getting faster, with winning race times getting much quicker since the turn of the century.

A leading veterinary scientist named Dr Sharman analysed the times of horses running on the flat between 1850 and 2012. Interestingly he found that there had been little improvement in speeds between 1910 and 1975, but since then there has been a steady improvement in sprint race times, with most of the improvement coming since the turn of this century. For example, in the past decade he found that the average winning time for a six-furlong race had been cut by more than a second - a huge margin when you consider that one second equals five lengths in a sprint. Dr Sharman calculated that a sprinter today would beat a sprinter from the 1990s by seven horse lengths.

According to Dr Sharman the improvement could be explained by a change in riding techniques since the 1970s - with jockeys adopting Lester Piggott's style of riding with shortened stirrups. The improvement could also be explained by improved training methods. Breeding also matters, but to a lesser extent.

Recent scientific research shows that the modern jockeyship and training methods have improved the racehorse more so than breeding. Research by Dr Wilson and Dr Rambaut at the University of Edinburgh found that only 10 per cent of a horse's lifetime winnings can be attributed to their bloodline. The scientists compared the stud fees, winnings and earnings of more than 4,000 racehorses since 1922. They found that while genes mattered to some extent, how the horse was trained, the choice of races entered and which jockeys were employed seemed to matter much more. The racehorse is therefore still a racehorse, but environmental factors have exerted more and more of an influence on how the average racehorse performs.

What does this mean for the punter in the twenty-first century? It suggests to me that the ability of the jockey and the trainer now matter much more than they once did. Both have always been important factors but they now matter even more. Therefore the successful punter needs to understand more about whether a horse has been entered in the right type of race (i.e. in a race that meets the horses preferences), and that the horse has been placed in the right grade and is well-handicapped. This is because horses have their own characteristics and you need to understand what these are to know when a horse is most likely to win. For instance, if a horse likes soft ground, a strong pace and has only ever won in a certain grade of race then you need to be able to spot when these conditions hold because this will bring out the best in a horse. A lot of this information can be gleaned from the form book, provided that you know where to look.

You also need to understand, like a good trainer, whether the horse is fit and well. Horses do have a ‘winning look’ and you can spot some signs of when a horse might win (or when it won't) by looking for clues in the paddock parade before the race or as the horse goes down to the start.

In this chapter we consider how we can identify a horse characteristics and it's preferences, and how we can profit from this information.

Can horses adapt to new race conditions?

Despite writing a book about the changes that have impacted on horse racing and betting in the twenty-first century I'm personally not a big fan of change. Some might say that this is because I'm at a certain stage of life. You know the one. The balding, fat and post-forty phase. The fact is though I've never really liked change. The adventure of foreign travel to me has always been stressful. Why waste your precious holiday time by going somewhere new when you know the place you went last year will be hard to beat? For the same reasons I also like to eat at the same restaurants when I go out. The last time I tried anywhere new I got food poisoning. For these reasons I'm suspicious of change, and especially when the only reason for making a change is because someone tells you 'it's time for a change'. Racehorses appear to share my view on life. Unfortunately their trainers keep on insisting that they need to embrace change and keeping trying out for them new race classes, new going or new distances. The data suggests that change is seldom profitable when it comes to horses encountering new race conditions. This seems to be a constant that is as true today as it was twenty years ago.

Trainers are always trying to do different things with horses that don't win races. My brief foray into racehorse ownership taught be this. When my quarter-tonne of prospective dog food raced for the first time it finished so far behind that a search party was dispatched. When I enquired into the poor run the trainer said that the ground was too soft. Next time out the horse ran on faster ground. When that change didn't work I was told that the distance was too short. Next time out a different distance was tried but in the post mortem for the also rans the trainer said that what was needed was a set of blinkers, then it was a tongue tie, then it was a soft palate operation, then finally it was the sales. I came to the conclusion that trainers need to constantly make changes in order to placate impatient owners, otherwise no one would stick with sinking thousands into racehorse ownership.

However, the astute punter can profit from this, especially when it comes to laying horses on the exchanges, because horses seem to take time to adapt to any new condition.

The statistics on horses changing distance between races show the pitfalls of betting on horses that are encountering a change in distance. My analysis tells me that, over hundreds of thousands of races over the jumps, handicap chasers and handicap hurdlers that run over roughly the same distance (i.e. experience a percentage change in distance between their current and previous race of no more than 20 per cent) win 9.8 per cent of the time. However, horses going up in distance by more than 20 per cent win only 7.7 per cent of the races that they contest while horses going down in distance by 20 per cent or more win at a rate of about 8.5 per cent. These difference in percentages may not sound much but when you think about it a horse running over pretty much the same distance is winning at a rate 1.28 times more than a horse going up in distance by 20 per cent or more. This is regardless of their ability or any other factor other than the change in distance between races.

The presence of new headgear is another powerful negative. In my opinion Nick Mordin in '*Betting for a Living*' gave a very plausible explanation as to why horses wearing blinkers win so infrequently, especially when racing in blinkers for the first time. He said that blinkers work because they prevent horses from seeing from behind. This makes them nervous of attack and their natural response is to flight. Consequently horses wearing blinkers for the first time run as if someone has set them on fire. The poor animal though soon becomes exhausted from this outburst of nervous energy, and this probably explains why they have such a poor win record. This pattern is particularly the race in flat racing over sprint distances (although to some extent it holds true over all distances).

A few years ago I did some research to show that that beaten favourite two-year olds record a strike rate of 41 per cent if they have been made favourite again and are not wearing blinkers or visors. However if they are wearing blinkers or visors for the first time then the strike rate falls alarmingly to just 29 per cent.

Another negative factor is whether or not the horse has changed trainer. When I did some research into juvenile beaten favourites I found that beaten favourites that had the same trainer did very well and won about 40 per cent of the races they contested but horses that switched trainers won at less than half this rate.

A further factor worth noting is whether or not the horse has recently been gelded. Recently gelded horses have an appalling win record especially if they have been gelded as a two-year old. This is hardly surprising when one considers the reasons as to why a colt might be gelded at such a tender age. Firstly, the colt is likely to be a bit of a rogue and has probably shown a tendency to have its mind on other things! Secondly, the decision has been made that the horse has no stallion potential. In other words connections believe that the horse is useless and that it wouldn't be worth its keep as a sire. Basically if you read in the Racing Post that a flat horse has been gelded since its last race then you are best to avoid it. The trend is the same in jump races although to a lesser extent.

Race class is another interesting angle. In Great Britain races are assigned a class level e.g. class 1, class 2, class 3 race etc. In jump races my analysis shows that horses running in the same class as their previous race win at a rate of 9 per cent. Horses going up 1 class level do a bit better and win at a rate of 9.9 per cent, but horses going up by more than that have a poor record and horses going up 2 or 3 class levels win at a rate of just 7 per cent. In contrast horses going down in class do very well. If they go down 1 level they win at a rate of 11 per cent; down 2 classes and they win at a rate of 15.6 per cent; and if they go down by more than that they win at a rate of about 23 per cent. Therefore horses going up in class can tolerate a small change in class but a bigger step up is often beyond them despite the pre-race optimism of trainers and owners that think they are up to the challenge.

There are occasions when a horse might cope well with a change. For instance, they might move to a better trainer and this might result in improved performance. However, my observations are that this seldom takes place on the horses first outing for the new trainer. Indeed, the data presented above suggests that horses do not cope well with change. A change in race conditions often means that the horse will need to adapt to the new class, pace and stamina requirements of the contest. They may do this eventually but they take time to acclimatise. The statistics seem to suggest that you would either be best to avoid backing horses that are attempting something different from their previous race or think about laying them on the exchanges.

Is the horse well handicapped?

The racing programme is now full of handicap races because they generate more revenue and profits for bookmakers, and some of this money goes back into the racing industry. This has been one of the key changes in the racing game this century and it has been a challenge for some punters.

Fortunately for me handicaps are now one of my favourite races to bet in. This wasn't the case in my early years in racing. In those days I used to think that the best way to make my betting pay was to only ever bet in non-handicaps. My logic was sound enough. I reasoned that it was hard enough working out the best horse in a race. The extra complexity of then having to work out which horse was the best off at the weights sounded like a step too far. These days I'm more open minded and I treat handicap races as interesting puzzles, and far more rewarding than completing the days Sudoku in my morning newspaper!

Handicap races also form the vast majority of a day's racing, especially over jumps. Strict adherence to a policy of only betting in non-handicaps over the sticks would mean that you would end up betting far too often than is good for you in novice chases and juvenile hurdle races. The other advantage of betting in handicaps in jump races is that most horses have exposed form. In other words each horse has ran a number of times and so you have a far idea of how good are horse is and some idea of its preferred conditions in terms of track, going, jockey and distance. is made up by such races. This is help from a form perspective and it helps to take out a bit of the guesswork when studying a race because you basically have more evidence to work with.

The paradox though is that if we punters have plenty of form to work with then the same also applies to the official handicapper. It could therefore mean that the handicapper is able to frame a race so that all horses have an equal chance of winning, if they all run to the best of their ability. The competition is therefore between the punter and the handicapper, and who can read the form the best. The obvious key to a handicap is to identify the horse that has a level of ability that is greater than the official handicappers assessment. For example, you would say that a horse is well handicapped if you give it a rating of 140 but the handicapper gives the horse an official rating of 130. Provided that you are both using the same handicapping scale then you are saying that the horse is ten pounds better than the horse's official rating. In a handicap of two miles or more over jumps, an advantage of ten pounds would be the equivalent of a ten length advantage.

An important difference between the official handicap ratings and those produced by the Racing Post or some other handicap ratings service is that the official handicap rating is a measure of what the BHA think is the underlying ability of the horse whereas the Racing Post Ratings (RPR) is an assessment of the horse's performance in a given race. This is an important distinction and explains why you often see a horse rated, say, 140 by the official handicapper but with a RPR in its last race well below that figure. This difference will show that the horse underperformed last time out, and ran below its official level of ability. In contrast a horse may sometimes receive an RPR in excess of its official rating. This isn't that common when comparing a horses recent RPR figures to the official rating because the official handicapper will obviously raise a horses handicap rating if they are progressing and performing well. However, it can happen when a horse runs to a high RPR figure, and looks like it will be raised in the official ratings.

Trainers attempt to cash in when this happens and try to get another run into an improving horse before the official handicapper has had a chance to review his ratings. A more common occurrence is when a horse has an official rating well below its best level of form. For example, a horse might now have an official rating of 100 but 12 months ago the horse turned in a performance of 120 on RPR ratings. At the time the horse might also have been running off a higher official handicap rating, and has now been dropped in the weights. The question for the punter is whether or not the horse will return to a level of performance that would earn it another 120 figure or whether the horse is deteriorating or that peak figure was a fluke. If the horse can indeed run back up to near its peak level of form then you will have identified a horse that is very well handicapped. You will be betting on a horse that could be as much as 20 pounds better off at the weights for the day's race. Identifying horses in this situation can result in big pay days because they will often go off at along price.

I've conducted some analysis of Racing Post Ratings or RPRs on National Hunt handicap races to try to identify when a horse might look to be well handicapped. I've gone through the form of each horse in my database and recorded their maximum RPR figure from all their previous races. I've then recorded the number of days (compared to their current race) since the horse earned its maximum figure.

In Figure 1 below I've plotted the relationship between the number of days since a horses maximum RPR and the % strike rate. It makes for interesting reading. It shows that horses making a quick return to the track since recording a top RPR won at a rate of 30% plus if returning to the track within seven days. This might be because trainers are looking to exploit a high rating before the handicapper increases his official rating for the horse (official ratings are updated on a weekly basis). After seven days the strike rate falls steadily. I've not plotted it here but eventually the line becomes pretty flat after 100 days. This suggests that top form ratings earned more than a year ago are worth about as much as one earned 100 days ago. This all suggests that punters need to focus on horses with a top figure within 7 days or between 8 and 25 days. After that it has less value. This doesn't mean to say that this is the horse's most recent figure. It may have disappointed a couple of times since earning a top figure. It looks from the data that a horse is more likely to run back up towards a decent figure (i.e. a winning one) if it's best previous performance was in the recent past.

Figure 1: Winning strike rate and days since previous best RPR rating, NH handicaps races only.

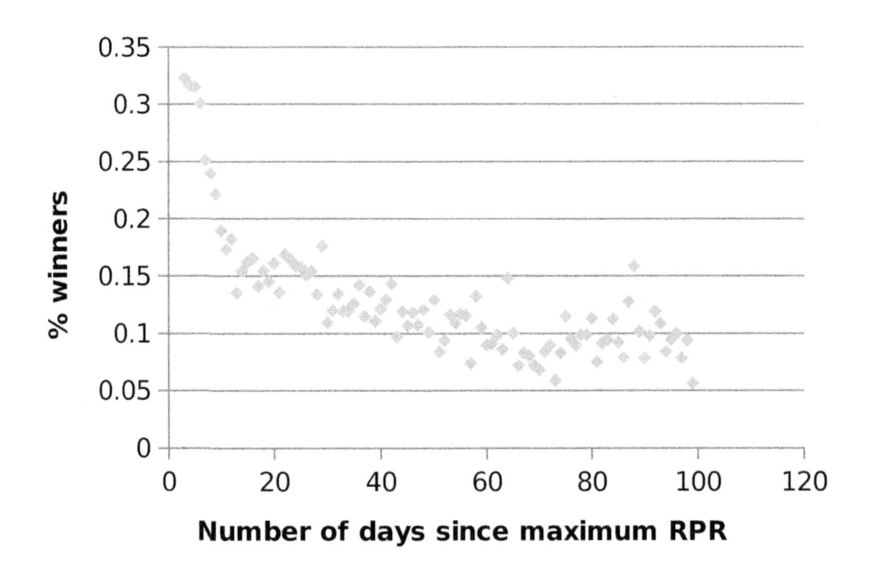

I then looked to see if there was a relationship between the winning strike rates of horses that had a maximum RPR in excess of their official rating. My reasoning would be that a horse that had a maximum rating in excess of its official rating could be well handicapped and therefore these horses should have a higher winning strike rate in handicaps than horses that have a current official handicap rating higher than their best RPR. The results are pretty conclusive.

Figure 2 shows that horses that have an official rating 6 pounds higher than their best RPR win at a rate of around 5 per cent. Horses that have an official rating equal to their best RPR win at a rate of 8 per cent.

Horses that are at least 6 pounds ahead of the handicapper on RPRs win at around 11 per cent or more than twice as often as those horses that a six pounds 'wrong' at the weights. Note: I've confined this analysis to a range of -6 to +6 pounds to give very large samples within this range.

Figure 2: Winning strike rate of horses with higher or lower official ratings compared to their best RPR

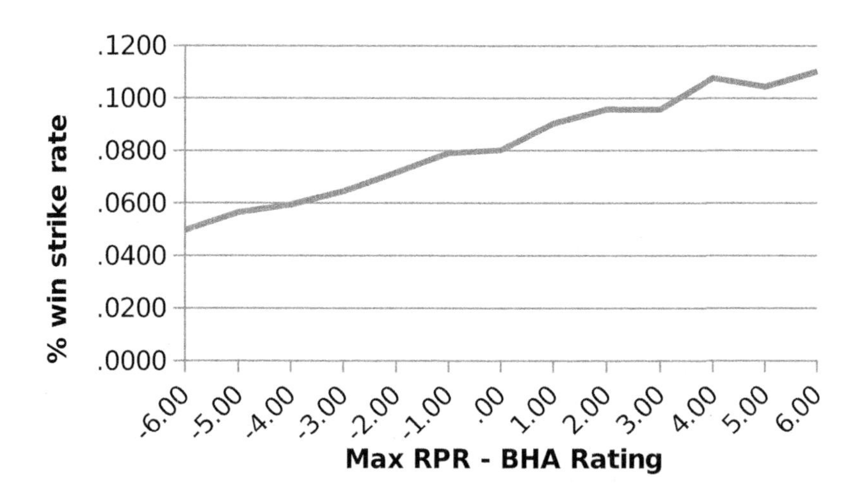

I think there are some interesting findings here and the bones of a winning betting strategy. The data seems to suggest that horses with higher RPRs than their official ratings are more likely to win. However, RPR ratings seem to decay with time. It is no good finding a horse that is 20 or 30 pounds better off on its best form compared to its current official rating if those career best figures were earned years ago. Indeed horses with a top RPR figure within the last 7 days are worth particular attention and those returning to the track with a top figure within 25 days also look like good candidates. Horses with a top figure of more than 100 days ago are probably unlikely to return to that level of form.

Can a horse still win despite being 'out of the handicap'?

Almost everyday when I'm either watching the horse racing or reading the Racing Post I hear or read the comment that a horse has absolutely no chance if it is racing 'out of the handicap'. I decided to load up my laptop, put on the kettle, and get my database up and running to test to see if this is actually true.

When a horse runs outside of the handicap it means that it cannot run off the correct weight for its official rating . All horses – flat or jumping – have official ratings set of the British Horse racing Authority (BHA). These ratings are used to set a handicap weight for each horse in handicap races. The race conditions will also stipulate a minimum weight for the race and this is usually set at a minimum of 10 stones over jumps.

Handicap races will also be limited to horses with a certain handicap rating. For example, the conditions for a three mile and two furlong handicap hurdle at Catterick on 23rd November 2018 state that the race is for horses rated by the official handicapper between zero and up to 115. The minimum weights is set at 10 stones. The top weight is a horse called Our Reward who has a handicap rating of 116 (a recent rule changes means that horses that are one or two pounds higher than the maximum official rating are still eligible to run). He is set a weight of 11 stones and 12 pounds. At the other end of the handicap Shaiyzar has a rating of 85. That is 31 pounds below the top weight Our Reward.

Our Reward has a weight of 11 stones and 13 pounds (or 167 pounds in weight) but Shaiyzar is set the minimum weight of 10 stone or 140 pounds. The difference in weight between them is therefore 27 pounds, but the difference between them on official ratings is 31 pounds. This means that Shaiyzar is carrying four pounds more than he should based on his BHA ability rating, and this is called being four pounds out of the handicap. Had the handicap not had a minimum weight of 10 stones then Shaiyzar should have carried 9 stones and 10 pounds but because jockeys cannot be expected to ride at weights much below 10 stone in National Hunt racing then Shaiyzar has to carry more weight than he really should. If you believe that every pound of weight makes a difference of one length in a handicap hurdle over an extended three miles, then Shaiyzar is starting with a four length disadvantage compared to all his rivals that have been set the correct weight according to their official handicap ratings.

Expressed in these terms then Shaiyzar is at a serious disadvantage compared to all the other horses in the race as he is effectively giving them all a significant head start. If one assumes that the handicap system works to equalise the difference between all the runners then being four pounds 'wrong' at the weights should mean, all other things being equal, that Shaiyzar has no chance. Of course the reality could be very different, One school of thought in racing is that handicap weights really don't make too much difference as the difference a few pounds makes to the outcome of a race is probably too small to make any material difference, especially when one considers that an average racehorse probably weighs around a-quarter-of-a-tonne. A few extra pounds on its back is hardly likely to be noticed.

Trainers might also mitigate the effect of being 'wrong' at the weights by employing the services of a good claiming jockey that can take a few extra pounds off the horses weight, and the claim might be sufficient to put the horse back into the proper handicap. The trainer might also know that the horse is actually a bit better than its official handicap rating and may therefore have decided to run the horse in the race, even if it is out of the handicap, on the basis that it won't be too inconvenienced by the extra burden. The advantage of being out of the handicap might also be enough to put others punters off and for the trainer and connections of the horse to secure a better price than they might otherwise have done so.

What does the data tell us about these different theories? My database records horses running out of the handicap and the number of pounds that they are 'wrong' at the weights. I considered all handicap jump races run other fences or hurdles since 2010 to give a big enough sample to make reliable conclusions.

Horses than run at the correct weight are shown to win at a rate of about 11 wins per 100 races (10.8%). However, horses that run out of the weights win at a rate of 9 per cent. This is a bit lower than the random probability, suggesting that being out of the handicap is a slight disadvantage. Given this one would expect horses running out of the handicap by more than five pounds to have an even worse strike rate because they are presumably at a bigger disadvantage than horses racing 'wrong' at he weights by four pounds or less. This though isn't the case and horses that are five pounds or more 'wrong' win at almost the same rate as horses four pounds of less out of the handicap.

This data suggests that being out of the handicap probably isn't too much of a disadvantage and if it is a disadvantage then other factors might offset the effect because the trainer might still run the horse because it is ahead of the handicapper, or is able to offset the disadvantage by using a jockey who can claim a weight allowance.

Punters though may be put off backing a horse if it isn't 'right' at the weights and this might create a bit of value to those that don't think that being out of the handicap really matters. This sounds like a plausible strategy but the statistics tell a different tale. At Betfair Starting Prices (taking into a account a 5% commission rate on all winning returns), if you bet a level stake on every horse that was racing off its correct weight, then you would lose 2.8% of all stakes invested. Betting horses that are out of of the handicap would lose you slightly more money. Betting to a level stake at the BSP on all horses out of the weights would result in a loss of 3.3%, which isn't very different from the 2.8% you would lose by betting on horses running off their correct weight.

In summary, horses that race out of the handicap are not a significant disadvantage compared to horses that race off the correct weight. The strike rate and level of loss at level stakes is more or less the same for the two groups. In other words the next time you see a horse running out of the handicap you shouldn't automatically discard it. It has no better or worse chance than any other runner in the race.

Can you predict which horse will set the early pace?

In my first book *Pace Wins The Race* I gave a very detailed account of how you could identify horses that were most likely to set the early pace. That book is now more than fifteen years old but the methods in it have stood the test of time, which is rare in the ever evolving world of horse racing.

The reason why you can predict which horses are likely to set the early pace is that in terms of running styles horses tend to be creatures of habit. From the coding of the comments recorded in the form book it is possible to predict, with a reasonable level of precision, which horses are likely to take the lead, based on how they have run in the past.

A horse that has taken an early lead in a previous race is more likely to do so in the future. It may not display the same running style in all its races, but it will display the style often enough for us to have a degree of confidence that it may show the same behaviour again.

I made this observation from the fact that horses who do not show any evidence of early pace in their previous three races race up with the pace in only 32 per cent of the races that they contest (see Table below). In contrast horses that show pace on each of their last three runs are more likely than not to show pace in their next outing (53 per cent).

Number of previous races where horse shows early pace and probability of horse showing early pace on next start.

Number of previous races showing early pace	Pacers	Runners	% pace
0	52,663	167,036	31.5
1	34,201	94,183	36.3
2	29,920	65,722	45.5
3	12,103	22,958	52.7

On the basis of this analysis I was able to make a simple prediction about which horses were more likely to take the lead. I reasoned that a horse that showed pace in each of its last three starts was a shade of odds-on to do so again.

However, this method is a very crude measure of pace. It is a crude method because all of the key race comments used to define pace ("tracked" or "chased" leaders, "led/leader to halfway", "made all", raced "prominent", raced in the "front rank") are assumed to be of equal predictive value. In other words it is assumed that a horse that earned the comment “chased leaders” on their last performance is just as likely to race up with the pace in their next race as a horse that received the comment “made all”. I can tell you, from an exhaustive analysis, that not all the comments in the form book are of equal value in this respect, and one needs to take this into account when making a prediction about whether the horse will show pace in their future races.

In the Figure below it can be seen that horses that “lead at half way” or who “made all” were the most likely to show pace again in their next race. Horses that merely chased the leaders or who raced prominently were less likely to repeat the behaviour, although a respectable proportion did so. This is to be expected. Horses that race only prominently or who chase or track the leaders are probably not complete tearaways like those that prefer to race in the ‘front rank’ or enjoy taking an outright lead.

Pace comments from previous races and probability of showing early pace on next start.

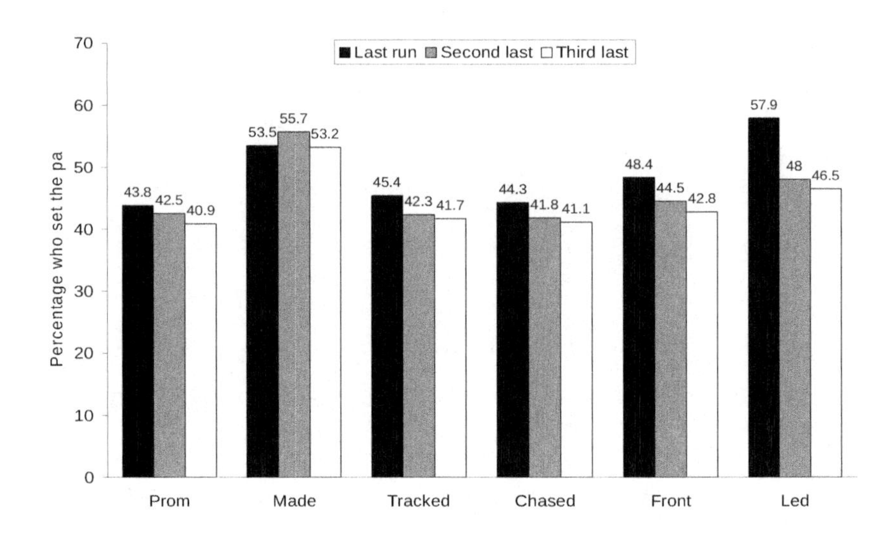

The predictive merit of each comment though is also shown to decline with the passage of time. I have found that a horse that made all in its last race is more likely to show pace again than a horse that recorded the same comment on its second and third last runs. In other words if you see a horse that earned the comment "made all" in all of its last three races it is the fact that it "made all" in is last race that is the most significant piece of information.

Therefore, when making a prediction about a horse's running style, you need to take account of the fact that not all comments are equal, and comments from more recent races are more likely to be repeated than older ones. These facts can be taken into account in a point scoring system to predict which horse is likely to show early pace.

There are a whole number of different types of comments reported in the form book but fortunately they are compiled using a common reporting style, and use a limited number of expressions. It is this that makes it possible to define early pace in a consistent manner and to statistically analyse the reported comments. From analysing these comments I have developed a list of six common expressions that are used to describe when a horse shows early pace, namely:

- "Prominently"
- "Made all"
- "Tracked leaders"
- "Chased leaders"
- "Front rank"
- "Led/leader to halfway"

I have programmed my computer to categorise all 'comments in running' into these six pace categories. The computer does this by scanning all the words in the 'comments in running' line for each horse and identifying key words. For example, if it reads the line 'Made all, easily' it notes the words 'made all' and categorises the horse as showing early pace by placing it in the 'made all' pace category. The word 'easily' is ignored.

A horse that has recorded any one of the above six pace comments in it's three previous races is a better than even money shot to show the same behaviour again. My statistics show that 53 per cent of horses with this profile show early pace in their next race. In contrast only 32 per cent of horses that showed no evidence of early pace in their previous races went on to show early pace in their next race.

Number of previous races where horse shows early pace and probability of horse showing early pace on next start.

Number of previous races showing early pace	% pace
0	31.5
1	36.3
2	45.5
3	52.7

However, this method is a very crude way to predict early pace because all of the race comments ("tracked" or "chased" leaders, "led/leader to halfway", "made all", raced "prominent", raced in the "front rank") are assumed to be of equal predictive value. In other words it is assumed that a horse that earned the comment "chased leaders" on their last performance is just as likely to race up with the pace in their next race as a horse that received the comment "made all". I can tell you, from an exhaustive analysis, that not all the comments in the form book are of equal value in this respect, and one needs to take this into account when making a prediction about whether the horse will show pace in their future races. I take this into account in my point scoring system to predict which horse is likely to show early pace.

My basic point scoring system gives each comment in the form book a weight according to its value in predicting whether a horse will show early pace. It is based on the horse's last three performances, and the higher the final score the more likely the horse is to show early pace.

A scoring system to predict early pace is not an original idea. William Quirin first proposed it in the 1970s in his study into the effect of early pace on the results of races run in the United States. The method was revisited and adapted more recently by Nick Mordin in his book *'Betting for a living'* to apply to British racing. My scoring system though is different from that of both Querin and Mordin in that it is based on an exhaustive analysis of thousands of individual racing performances, and has been generated from some fairly advanced statistical methods.

In my basic pace scoring system I award points for the following comments:

Points to be awarded for pace comments

Pace comment	Last run	Second last run	Third last run
Led to halfway	8	5	3
Made all	7	4	3
Prominent	5	3	2
Tracked leaders	5	3	2
Chased leaders	4	3	2
Front rank	3	2	1

You will see that the maximum number of points that can be awarded is 16 points. A horse that scores above 10 points probably has a better than even money chance of setting the pace in it's next race.

Sometimes a horse will not necessarily have three previous rateable performances in the form book. I used to address this bias by imputing scores for the horses missing races from the pace scores that the horse had actually recorded. However, I no longer do this because I found that horses need to establish a proven record of early pace before they can be relied upon to show the behaviour again.

In summary my analysis demonstrates that in terms of running styles horses tend to be creatures of habit. A horse that has taken an early lead in a previous race is more likely to do so in the future. It may not display the same running style in all its races, but it will display the style often enough to assume that it will show the same style of running again.

Profiting from pace ratings

The pace scoring system that I reported above initially appears to be a rather crude tool but it is actually based on an exhaustive analysis of thousands of racing performances, and a sophisticated statistical model has generated the scores. The basic method outlined here has been improved upon by me in recent years. I now include allowances for whether the horse is wearing blinkers for the first time or is experiencing a change in race distance. The ratings are now available everyday for all flat races on www.profitablebetting.co.uk. Eventually I'll build into the model sectional time data, but unfortunately that form of data is only a very recent development in British racing, and is currently only available for some tracks (I'll discuss sectional time data later in this Chapter).

How can you profit from the current ratings? The pace ratings can be profitable as part of a back-to-lay strategy on the betting exchanges. My betting method is very simple. I use the my pace ratings to identify those horses that are most likely to set the early pace, and I back them to win prior to the race. If they perform as expected in the actual race and take an early lead then the 'in-play' odds on the selection tend to plummet. I then lay the selection to lose at the shorter price to a certain stake, and thereby ensure that I make a profit regardless of the race outcome. This is what is called a simple back-to-lay strategy because I'm backing a horse before the race on the expectation that I will lay it to lose during the race at shorter price.

The method is best described with an example from my database. My data tells me that the average Betfair SP on my predicted pacesetters is around 18.1. This is a fairly high average BSP because my methods aim to identify the horse most likely to set the pace, and not the horse most likely to win the race. The important thing to note here is that it is important to obtain the best possible back odds before the off on the selection because this gives the headroom to lay the horse for a profit when the race goes 'in-play' (I use the BSP as a proxy for the price available before the off, although better odds may have been available).

For the trading strategy to be successful the odds on the selection need to fall significantly when the race goes 'in-play'. The data is clear on this. The odds typically fall from an average BSP of 18.1 to an average low price 'in-play' of around 15.5 across all selections. This represents a price contraction of 15 per cent. Furthermore, the price contraction of 15 per cent includes those horses that the ratings predicted would set the pace, but who failed to do so. When these selections are removed from the analysis the price contraction is significantly greater at around 40 per cent.

When the odds fall on the horse that I have backed, I then make a quick calculation about how much to lay, and then enter the market to lay the same horse at the lower odds. This means that I now make a profit if the horse wins the race and if it loses, and I lay to stakes that ensure that I make an equal profit on either side of the bet regardless of the outcome. I won't go into this calculation now but in practice you can save yourself the maths lesson and buy-in or obtain for free specialist exchange trading software that can do the calculations for you, and place the bets for you into the exchange.

I'll illustrate how I make a profit by using an example I've randomly picked from my betting records from the last decade. The race in question is the 19.30 at Wolverhampton on the 8th February 2013. According to my ratings Illustrious Forest is highly likely to set the early pace. He's available to back at odds of 7.00 at the off. On my back bet of £10 I stand to make a profit of £60 if my selection wins the race. However, I'm not interested in whether the horse wins or loses. I'm interested in laying the same horse when the race goes 'in-play'.

The race now begins and my average selection does the business and takes an early lead. The 'in-play' markets now start buzzing and the odds fall to a low of just 2.00 because Illustrious Forest looks likely to hold on to his early lead, although there are still a couple of furlongs to go before the finish. I now lay the horse for £35 at decimal odds of 2.00 and the bet gets matched. If the horse wins my liability is £35. I now can't fail to make a profit regardless of the race outcome. I've made a profit of £25 whether the horse wins or loses (minus commission). Illustrious Forest makes a brave effort to make all, but tires inside the final furlong to eventually finish second. However, I'm not cursing like other punters that may have backed him to win. I've still won on the race thanks to my pace ratings and my back-to-lay trading strategy.

How did I make £25 on this race? My liability on my lay bet i.e. the amount of money I would have had to pay out to 'in-play' punters had the horse won was £35. This though was £25 less than the £60 that I would have made had the horse won. On the other side of the bet when Illustrious Forest lost I lost all of my £10 back stake on him, but I collected the £35 that I took from the 'in-play' punters who backed him with me at odds of 2.00 (or evens). Therefore when the horse lost I still made £25 (£35 - £10).

This though isn't easy money and it isn't a guaranteed profit. Profitability rests on your skill and judgement as a trader, and you need to develop these skills for yourself if you want to make your pace strategy successful. For instance, in the above example Illustrious Forest led from the start and as the race went on his odds contracted. Had I bottled it when the odds first started to fall then I might have taken a lay bet at 4.00 or 3.00 etc. I would still have made a profit because my back price was higher, but I wouldn't have made the full £25. In order to maximise profits you need to get a feel for when the 'in-play' price is about to turn and get out before it does. This takes experience, but once you have this you are on your way to making a steady and consistent profit from your trades.

The key thing to note is that the lay bet may go wrong and the 'in-play' price may not go lower than the back price. In this situation you just have to sit and suffer and write the back bet off as a loss or trade out to minimise losses.

The bottom line is that after taking into account these losses my results show that, based on optimal trading (i.e. trading out at the lowest price 'in-play'), you can make a very decent profit from a relatively simple strategy based around my pace ratings.

Making use of sectional time data

The pace ratings I have described above have the advantage in that they are available for every race in the UK and Ireland because they make use of 'comments-in-running' data that is freely available in the form book. They could of course be improved if sectional times data was available for every race. Despite this being the twenty-first century sectional times data is still not routinely available for every race. However, I need to give a shout out for the innovation shown by attheraces.com and Sky television to go into partnership with a company called Total Performance Data in order to provide sectional times at all the 18 tracks covered by Sky Racing.

This development is especially commendable because the data is available for free from the atheraces.com website. The website also provides detailed metrics on the pace in each part of the race and the speed of each horse in each section. It can do this because of the excellent technology developed by Total Performance Data that basically puts a GPS tracker in the saddle cloth of each horse. This allows the horses to be tracked in the same way that the satnav is your car is tracked (I simplify greatly here but if you are interested full details are available from totalperformancedata.com). This has to be much more accurate than hand-timed sectional times recorded by some punters and commercial companies from video replays.

The coverage of the attheraces.com/Sky service has gradually extended overtime. The project initially covered just the four ARC owned all-weather racecourses (Lingfield, Newcastle, Southwell and Wolverhampton) and was launched at the start of the 2016-17 All-Weather Championships. Later in 2017 the coverage of sectional times was extended to also cover flat racing at Doncaster and Windsor, and from May 2018 the service was extended again to all flat meetings at Bath and Chepstow.

In April 2019 the service was extended again to cover flat racing at Brighton, Ffos Las and Yarmouth and then in November 2019 sectional times were also made available on the atheraces.com website for certain jump courses. These included Bangor-on-Dee, Chepstow, Doncaster, Ffos Las, Fontwell, Hereford, Lingfield, Newcastle, Sedgefield, Southwell, Uttoxeter and Worcester.

Sadly the coverage of the service still only covers a minority of all the racecourses in the UK (although in terms of all-weather racing only Kempton and Chelmsford are missing) and so the service is far from comprehensive but I still think there is a lot to be learned from this new dataset and I've started to analyse the data.

The first thing I looked at was the average speed of race winners at different sections of a race and the results are recorded in the Table below.

There are several things to note about this data. The average speed recorded by the race winner over the entire distance of the race is greater than for the distance up to the 4 furlong marker. This is pretty obvious because horses will need time to accelerate from the start until they reach a cruising speed. However, once you ignore the starting sectional and consider only the last 3 furlongs of the race you begin to note something about how races are run.

The winner is clocking a top speed between the 3 and 1 furlong markers, but then decelerates in the final furlong. To novice racegoers this seems an odd finding because one might assume that horses are running fastest at the end of a race. The actual story though is that horse races are all about the optimum use of energy. A horse that runs too fast in the early stages or final few furlongs will pay the price in the final furlong. However, it can get away with this as long as it has a big enough lead at that point, or is fit enough to be decelerating less than the other runners.

The other thing to note about the Table below is that when you look at average speeds by race class you see see bigger differences in the speed of the horses by the official race class over the last three furlongs than in comparison to the overall speed recorded by the horses over the whole race distance, and certainly than over the earlier part of the race.

The data shows that Class 1 horses have an average speed nearly 2 miles per hour faster than class 7 horses between the 3 furlong and 2 furlong markers; the difference is just over 2 miles per hour from the 2 furlong to 1 furlong marker; and from the final furlong marker to the finish the class 1 winner clocks a speed of 1.65mph faster than the class 7 horse. However, because horses are typically decelerating in the final furlong, the relative difference in speed between class 1 and class 7 horses is around 5 per cent in each sectional split

Table: Average speed (mph) over difference race sections and by official race class

Race Section	Race Class	Mean (MPH)
Overall race	1	36.68
	2	36.59
	3	36.52
	4	36.26
	5	36.15
	6	36.02
	7	36.23
Start to 4f	1	34.35
	2	34.18
	3	34.13
	4	34.1
	5	34.14
	6	34.53
	7	34.64
3f to 2f	1	39.8

Race Section	Race Class	Mean (MPH)
	2	39.38
	3	39.34
	4	38.9
	5	38.43
	6	37.93
	7	37.87
2f to 1f	1	39.5
	2	39.36
	3	39.19
	4	38.58
	5	38.39
	6	37.65
	7	37.45
1f to finish	1	37.27
	2	37.54
	3	37.07

Race Section	Race Class	Mean (MPH)
	4	36.35
	5	36.44
	6	35.85
	7	35.59

The analysis above is a bit crude because I've lumped together all the attheraces.com sectional times data together and then pulled out a few statistics. Do I see the same pattern if I only concentrate on all-weather racing?

The Table below shows that the class trend is more significant in all-weather racing, and that you get progressively bigger differences over the last three race sections. For example in the final furlong of an all-weather race the class 1 winner is clocking a speed more than 3 seconds faster than the class 7 horse, which is around 8 per cent more. There are big differences over the other latter sections of a race but the class difference seems to be greatest in the critical final furlong, even though the horses are recording lower speeds over this furlong than over the preceding 2 furlongs.

Table: Average speed (mph) over difference race sections and by official race class, all-weather only.

Race Section	Race Class	Mean (MPH)
Over race	1	36.68
	2	36.59
	3	36.52
	4	36.26
	5	36.15
	6	36.02
	7	36.23
Start to 4f	1	34.35
	2	34.18
	3	34.13
	4	34.1
	5	34.14
	6	34.53
	7	34.64
3f to 2f	1	39.8

Race Section	Race Class	Mean (MPH)
	2	39.38
	3	39.34
	4	38.9
	5	38.43
	6	37.93
	7	37.87
2f to 1f	1	39.5
	2	39.36
	3	39.19
	4	38.58
	5	38.39
	6	37.65
	7	37.45
1f to finish	1	37.27
	2	37.54

Race Section	Race Class	Mean (MPH)
	3	37.07
	4	36.35
	5	36.44
	6	35.85
	7	35.59

Finally, when we consider only all-weather races run over a distance of a mile or less we see the same pattern as the above. The speed of the horse in the final furlong seems to be the best discriminator of a class 1 and a class 7 horse, and that this is far more significant than the speed recorded in the opening fraction or the overall race time. This give rise to a number of ideas. It would be interesting to mine the data a bit further to see whether the average speed of a horse in the final furlong or final three furlongs is a better predictor of class and future winners than the speed figures that are recorded over the race as whole. This indicator might flag horses that are under-rated and might progress in their future races.

Horses that show power in the final furlong

Sectional times data can also tell you which horse has finishing power.

I've analysed the speed of horses in the final furlong. This is often the slowest section of a race but my reasoning is that horses that clock the fastest time in the final furlong have that bit of extra power to mark them down as resolute stayers, or horses with a bit of extra class to mark them down as potential future winners.

In my analysis the horse that clocked the fastest speed in mph in the final furlong is ranked number one. I also do the same for the the last three furlongs of the race. I then analysed the performance of horses ranked number one in each sectional split on their next outing to see if the rankings identified future winners.

The statistics show that the horse that clocked the fastest time from the start to the four furlong marker won 14 per cent of the races that they contested next time out. However, when we focus on the last three furlongs of the race, which is usually the business end of a race, the figures look a bit more impressive. The fastest horse between the 3 furlong and 2 furlong marker won at a rate of 16 per cent next time out, and the horse that ran fastest between the 2 furlong and 1 furlong marker won at a rate of 18.4 per cent. What about the crucial final furlong? The horse that was fastest in this final split won at a rate of 19.4 per cent next time out.

The above analysis seems to suggest that the fastest horse in the final furlong is more likely to win next time than horses that recorded the fastest split in other sections of the race. This information though seems to be more useful at certain courses, especially Southwell.

Horses that recorded the fastest time last time out in the final furlong won at a rate 23.8 per cent at Southwell. In contrast the strike rate at other courses for horses meeting our speed criteria was 17.4 per cent at Newcastle, 18.3 per cent at Wolverhampton and 19.8 per cent at Lingfield.

This research suggests that horses that put in a strong finish in the final furlong are more likely to win next time out, but particularly at Southwell over the courses slower Fibresand surface. Fibresand is made up of a mixture of sand and fibres. Southwell is the only track to use this surface and it is a very different type of going than other surfaces. It is deeper than Tapeta or Polytrack and puts more of an emphasis on stamina. It therefore places more importance on a horses ability to stay the trip and their overall level of fitness. The power that a horse shows in the final furlong of it's races might therefore be a stronger predictor of the horses stamina and ability to sustain a strong finish in the final furlong of a race.

Should you be wary of horses that win by wide margins?

Horses can deceive you, and horses that win by wide margins can be the most deceiving of all.

The statistics clearly show that backing wide margin winners in their next race is a short cut to the poor house. I've considered thousands of races in recent flat race seasons and while the strike rate of wide margin winners is better than average, punters almost always over bet them. The odds of horses that won last time by four lengths or more is considerably shorter than winners generally and you would record a loss of around 20 per cent on turnover (see Table below).

Profit and loss recorded by last time out winners, by winning distance (flat races only)

Winning distance from last race	Winner/ loser	Ave SP	N	Profit/ loss (£)	Profit/ loss (%)
Less than 1 length	loser	11.0	2,652		
	winner	4.7	410	-722.61	-0.24
	Total	10.2	3,062		
1 length, less than 2 lengths	loser	10.2	1,662		
	winner	4.2	304	-380.07	-19.33
	Total	9.3	1,966		
2 lengths, less than 3 lengths	loser	10.7	706		
	winner	3.9	147	-138.81	-0.16
	Total	9.5	853		
3 lengths, less than 4 lengths	loser	10.1	430		
	winner	3.5	81	-148.04	-0.29
	Total	9.1	511		
4 lengths or more	loser	10.8	528		
	winner	2.9	134	-135.36	-0.20
	Total	9.2	662		

Wide margin winners are often not good betting propositions and you should be extremely cautious of backing them as they often flatter to deceive.

Don't forget the horse's birthday: the significance of foaling dates

The last twenty years has seen more fixtures and racing than ever before. You simply can't bet on all of it and most professional punters that I know always give the same advice. They all say that you need to specialise in one area of racing, and get to know it, and really absorb yourself in the detail so that you know all there is to know about one specific aspect of the racing game. This will allow you to gain an edge over other punters and help you make a decent profit over the long term.

One area that definitely requires specialist skill is juvenile flat racing. This often gets the swerve from most punters because there is very little form to go on, with lots of unraced horses, and the results can often be unpredictable. There are though a few statistics that might help you gain the upper hand in this area of the game.

When betting on two-year olds a horse's breeding is probably the most important of all factors. The horse's sire, dam and grand sire provide the only real clues as to how a juvenile will perform in its early races. I'm therefore always surprised about the number of punters that completely ignore a horse's bloodline. This though is fortunate for those that bother to seriously study the pedigree of juveniles because it ensures that pedigree based bets can be placed at decent odds. I'd therefore strongly recommend that you stick to the horses that are well bred and in the hands of one of the top trainers. However, you still need an edge on these horses because you can't bet on all of them. You therefore need to be able to discriminate between them on one factor that other punters might ignore.

When betting in juvenile races, one of the most significant angles that I have found is the horse's birthday, or more specifically the month in which it was foaled. In the Table below I have re-produced my analysis of the win record of two year-olds by the month in which they were foaled.

Win record of juveniles that raced in Great Britain and Ireland, by month foaled

Month foaled	Winners	Runners	% Win
JAN	164	1,366	12.0
FEB	425	4,031	10.5
MAR	479	5,458	8.8
APR	455	5,587	8.1
MAY	103	1,760	5.9
JUN	1	42	2.4
DEC	-	3	0.0
Total	1,627	18,247	8.9

The data presented above clearly demonstrates a significant bias in favour of two-year-olds that were born in the early part of the year. For instance, juveniles that were born in the previous January won at a rate of 12 per cent but horses foaled in June won at a rate of 2.4 per cent. In other words juveniles foaled in January were five times more likely to win than those foaled in June.

This result is not surprising when one considers the administration of horse racing in Great Britain and Ireland, and how the authorities calculate horses racing age.

In these countries all racehorses share the same birthday, namely 1st January. This makes it easier for the authorities to calculate a horse's age because they do not have to find out the date of the horse's actual birthday. It does though create a major bias in two-year races because it means that a horse born on 1st June 2020 would be classified as a juvenile eligible for racing in January 2021, when their actual chronological age would be 19 months.

In comparison a horse actually born on 1st January 2020 would be 24 months on 1st January 2021, giving it an age advantage of five months over its more immature counterpart. Most trainers do not bother running June foals until they are officially three years of age in order to overcome this bias, and in the current sample few bothered to race horses that were born from July onwards.

The data above is clear that when betting in juvenile races one needs to concentrate on those runners that were foaled between the months of January and April, with preference being for those foaled in the months of January and February.

You will not find foaling date information in the racing pages of the main newspapers. You will have to obtain this information from sources such as the *Racing Post* website or some other specialist source.

If you stick to horses that are foaled early and also trained by the top trainers (e.g. top 20 in the current list of trainers) and sired by one of the top 20 sires (in terms of winners to runners) then you will do well in juvenile races. However, a note of caution. I've recently read that some breeders are working to ensure that more foals are born in the early months of the year to exploit the advantage that early foals have in juvenile races.

In the years ahead you might therefore see more early foals than you do now and this edge might be gradually be eroded for the punter. This is a good example of the challenges facing the punter in the modern age i.e. you find an edge and the racing world changes around it.

Watch out for weak finishers: assessing a horses going and distance preferences

Phil Bull, founder of Timeform and mega successful punter, once said that the most important factor when assessing any horse race is to work out which horse will act best on the going. There is perhaps more behind this statement than it first appears. After all when you think about a horses going preferences you are really saying something about a horses speed and stamina requirements. You are not actually saying that the horse will act on soft going because it has big feet! Sadly though I know of several punters that think along these lines when trying to work out whether a horse will act on the going. Unsurprisingly they all lose money!

It is the speed and stamina requirements that are posed by different types of going that first need to be understood. I have analysed thousands of handicap chases and handicap hurdle races and worked out the average number of seconds taken by the race winner to complete one furlong on different types of going. The results can be seen in the Table below.

Seconds take per furlong on different types of going

Chase

Going	**Seconds per furlong**	**Difference from average**
Firm	14.7	-0.9
Good-to-firm	14.9	-0.7
Good	15.2	-0.4
Good-to-soft	15.7	0.1
Soft	16.2	0.6
Heavy	16.6	1
All	15.6	

Hurdle

Going	**Seconds per furlong**	**Difference from average**
Firm	14.1	-1
Good-to-firm	14.3	-0.8
Good	14.7	-0.4
Good-to-soft	15.1	0
Soft	15.6	0.5
Heavy	16.3	1.2
All	15.1	

The Table above shows that an average three mile chase, over a distance of 24 furlongs, would take about one minute more to complete on heavy going than it would if the same race was run on a firm (sometimes called 'fast') surface. Basically over hurdles or fences heavy going adds about a second per furlong to race times. This is a pretty significant difference when you think that the average racecourse covers five lengths of distance per second. A horse that moves from firm to heavy going is going to be really slowed down by the underfoot conditions, and this is going to put a much greater emphasis on the horses stamina than had the race been run on firm ground. Conversely, a horse that moves from running on heavy ground to a fast surface is going to have to speed up by around 5 lengths per furlong. That is a lot of extra speed to find and the horse may simply not have the necessary zip to be competitive in that type of race.

Racehorse trainers might take a time to work out a horses going preferences but when they do they sometimes try to compensate for inadequate going by moving the horse up and down in race distance. This seems a logical thing to do. If you know your horse is better on heavy ground over three miles than over three miles on fast going then you might try to compensate by changing the horses race distance from three miles on heavy ground and giving it a try over three-miles-and-two-furlongs on good ground. The increase in distance, you would hope, might put more of an emphasis on the horses stamina.

I've done some analysis by looking at horses that earn the comment 'weakened' in the form book in their last race, and then seeing what happens to them next time out when the trainer changes either the race distance or going. The data is limited to handicap races only because this helps to control for differences in ability between horses.

The comment 'weakened' in the form book is interesting because it is often associated with a horse keeping up with the main contenders in a race but then gradually losing its position as other horses run past it, and it basically fades out of contention. In these situations the trainer might think that the horse weakened because the going and distance combination was wrong.

My analysis shows that horses that weakened in their last race but raced again at the same distance win at a rate of just over 8 per cent. However, horses that go up in distance win at a rate of just 6 per cent. This makes sense in that it must be harder for a horse that didn't look like it stayed last time out to then have to race over an even longer distance next time.

When you take out the effect of the going then the statistics make even more sense. A horse racing over the same going as before but going down in race distance, after a weak finish last time out, wins at a rate of 9 per cent, but when going up in distance wins at a rate of just 6 per cent. In addition a horse going up in distance and also running on softer going wins at a rate of just 5 per cent.

The thing that is interesting but harder to explain is why would a trainer watch a horse fade out of a race and then think that it needs both a longer trip and softer going next time out? Taking such action must surely increase the stamina required to win next time, and that looks like the quality that the horse lacks. These look like the horses to lay because it might be that the trainer is either trying to reduce the horses handicap mark by running it over the wrong ground and distance, or they are completely useless!

Basically look out for horses that are weak finishers in their races and watch the trainers next move with the horse, and avoid horses that are made to race over longer longer distances and softer ground.

Horses that 'stay on' at the finish

Despite it being the twenty-first century there is still a relative paucity of raw data in British horse racing. Certainly there is now plenty of information but this is mainly a secondary analysis of existing data in the form book. This isn't the same as in other countries. In contrast to our punting cousins in the USA and Hong Kong, the British punter is definitely the poor relation in terms of data.

In the USA and Hong Kong punters are treated to an array of raw data that we British punters can only dream about. For example, they have data on the weight of a horse each time it runs. For example if a horse weights 600 kilos in one race and is well beaten, 600 kilos in another race when again it is well beaten, and then races at a weight of 550kilos then the punter in Hong Kong knows that this time the horse is 50 kilos lighter and this would be evidence that the horse is much fitter than it was on either of its previous runs. This is important information.

Another useful source of data are sectional times. This data, despite it being the twenty-first century and the digital age, is still not routinely available for all British racecourses but in both the US and Hong Kong they have sectional timing for all flat races, and this is data is published in their equivalents of the Racing Post. Fortunately Sky Racing, attheraces.com and an innovative technology company called Total Performance Data teamed up in 2017 to at least provide sectional time data for some British all-weather tracks. The list of courses covered by this project was up to 18 in 2019 and all the data is published for free on the attheraces.com website.

However, the British Horse racing Authority and the rest of the mainstream racing media don't seem interested in investing in this new technology and making it available at every racecourse. This means that the US punter is much better off than their British counterparts because he or she has information on the time taken by every horse to complete each quarter mile section of a race., in every race in the US These sectional times provide invaluable information about how a race has been run and the level of pace. They also tell you something about the ability of a horse to stay on at the finish by comparing the time of the last quarter mile to the horses previous quarter distance times.

What can the British punter do about this? Not much to be honest. In addition to atheraces.com there are some sectional time services available that provide data on all races in the UK but these are hand timed figures taken from race recordings and therefore not as reliable as the service provided by atheraces.com, and the data needs to be paid for. There is no data on horse's weight, even though most if not all trainers weigh their horses regularly to see if they are fit. Therefore if, for example, you want to work out if a horse is seeing out its races well, there is no universal sectional times data and no data on whether the horse was fit enough to do itself justice in a finish.

The only freely available and fully comprehensive source of information about whether or not a horse is finishing off its races is the comments in the form book about the horse's performance during a race. These comment use a fairly standard vocabulary and regularly report horses as either 'stayed on' or 'stayed on well' which might suggest that the horse kept going in the finishing stages or had a surge late on in the race.

I’ve done some statistical analysis of the comments in the form book to see if they do indeed contain any winner finding information. I’ve looked at the data on handicap chase and handicap hurdle races since 2000 in Great Britain and Ireland and examined the comments in the form book on over 400,000 racehorse performances. I’ve done some statistical analysis of comments like ‘stayed on’ and ‘kept on’ that might suggest that a horse is performing well at the end of its races. This might suggest that the horse might be fit and is performing at its best. It might also suggest that the horse has been running over an inadequate distance and when going up in trip it might do the business.

The first thing to note in my analysis is that the comment ‘stayed on’ seems to be predictive of future winners. For example, horses that earned such a comment last time out won at rate of nearly 14% in their next race. In contrast horses that didn’t earn such a comment in their last race only won at a rate of 9 per cent when racing again next time. A 5 percentage point difference is a pretty big difference.

How though does the comment ‘stayed on’ compare to a comment like ‘kept on’? Both terms are very common in the form book. From my own observations of watching horse races over many, many years is that the comment ‘stayed on’ suggests a horse that is either closing in at the finish or wins a race by extending its advantage over its rivals in the final stages of a race. The term ‘kept on’ is encouraging but it suggests that the horse kept going at the same pace. It was probably neither losing nor gaining ground on its rivals at the finish, or won a race by basically keeping going and neither extended or conceded its advantage by the time it reached the winning post.

My statistics tell me that the comment ‘stayed on’ is more

predictive of next time out winner than the comment ‘kept on’ but that both are positive comments from a winner finding point of view, as both record more winners next time out than average. For instance, horses that earned the comment ‘kept on’ in their last race won at a rate of 10.5% in comparison to 9% for all other runners. This though isn’t as impressive as the 14% recorded by horses that received the comment ‘stayed on’ last time.

Another question is whether it is important, from a winner finding point of view, whether the horse earned the comment ‘stayed on’ in its last race or whether that comment is a positive for any previous race? The answer is that last time out form is better at predicting a winner next time than previous races. The respective winning strike rates of horses with the ‘stayed on’ comment in their last time, second last race and third last race was 14%, 12% and 11%. This would suggest that the comment is useful to see in at least one of the horses last three races as horses with these comments do better than the average runner, but that last time out form is the more important.

A really interesting finding from my analysis is the performance of horses that earned the comment ‘stayed on’ in their last race and then went up or down in distance next time out. Logic would suggest that if you have a horse that is staying on strongly at the end of a race but not winning then the trick might be to race it next time over a longer trip. I also know that in handicap races it is not unknown for a trainer to race a horse over an inadequate trip (i.e. short of its optimum) in order for it to get beaten a few times. It then goes down the official handicap scale. The trainer then races it over a longer and more appropriate trip and then wins the race thanks to the horses new lower handicap rating. This is all perfectly legitimate and part of racing. These cases can sometimes be picked up by a horse staying on at the finish of a previous race and then going up in trip.

What do the statistics tell us? They are pretty clear. A horse that earned the comment 'stayed on' and races next time over more or less the same distance (i.e. either exactly the same distance or plus or minus 20% of the previous race distance) win at a rate of 13.5% next time out. In contrast horses that go down in trip by more than 20% of the previous race distance win at a rate of just 12%. This is a fair bit worse than the average for all horses that earned the comment 'stayed on' and most be trained by trainers that are either blind or have some warped logic about the best distance for the horse. In contrast horses that earned the comment 'stayed on' but went up in distance by more than 20% won at a rate of 15%.

This fairly simple statistical analysis reveals that horses that earned the comment 'stayed on' last time out might have a better chance next time than the average runner. Their chance might be further improved by an increase in distance as the previous race was probably over an inadequate trip. In your systems and form analysis you might want to build these facts into your calculations.

The unlucky horse

There are a great number of betting systems on horse racing that are based around a horse's previous finishing positions. I recall that one of the first systems that I ever read was based around such a method.

The system cost me twenty-five quid and it involved awarding points according to where the horse had finished in its last two races. As you would expect the maximum number of points were awarded to the horse that had finished first in its last two starts. A horse could only score points if it had finished in the first four. No other form factors were considered

The simplicity of the system caused me concern. For instance, it didn't take into account whether the horse had finished first in a two horse race or had been placed fifth in a thirty runner handicap. Nevertheless, I was always surprised by how good the system was in helping to narrow down a field. I was recently thinking about whether this simple system could be improved to make it useful in the modern era.

The most obvious improvement to the system would be to normalise the finishing positions. This basically means putting them on to some sort of scale that takes into account the fact that races consist of different numbers of runners. The scale then allows one to make a valid statistical comparison between a horse that finishes second in a five runner race and a horse that finishes fifth of 30 runners.

A neat way to do this, taken from an old but excellent US racing book called *'Beating the Races With a Computer'* by Steven Brecher (published in 1980) is to re-compile form figures using the following formula:

0.5– (finishing position / number of runners in the race)

This creates a normalised finishing position. Thus a horse that finishes second in a race of five runners would get a figure of 0.1 because 2 divided by 5 is equal to 0.4. You subtract this figure from 0.5 and you arrive at a normalised figure of 0.1. However, had the horse finished third of five runners then the rating would be minus 0.1. In comparison if a horse finished fifth of 30 runners then the horse would have a normalised finishing position of 0.33. In other words finishing fifth of 30 runners (normalised figure of 0.33) is three times better finishing second of just five runners (0.1).

If you add up the normalised finishing position of a horses last two races then the horse with the highest score in a race has the best form figure rating. This might mean that the horse that finished fifth of 30 runners in its last race, and fifth of twenty runners in the race before that, is rated superior to a horse that won last time out beating two others runners and won the time before that beating five runners.

However, while normalised finishing positions can be used to compile useful form figure ratings, they are not the main focus here. Instead I want to use them to help quantify bad luck in running by calculating how many normalised finishing positions a horse might lose in a race if it had a bad start, was hampered in running or sustained some sort of injury in a race. This information, when combined with other factors, might prove to be useful and profitable because it would help to identify horses that appeared to run badly, and give some idea as to how much better they might have faired had they not experienced bad luck in running. This information could then be used to identify horses that might be overlooked by the betting public on their next outing.

In order to work out the amount of compensation owed to horses that had bad luck in running I had to use a statistical procedure called multiple regression. This basically works out the influence of different factors on a dependent variable. In this case the dependent variable is the normalised finishing position described above. I based the regression analysis on my database of over 900,000 performances, by thousands of horses that ran in flat races (turf and all-weather) in Great Britain and Ireland over the last decade.

The estimate of bad luck in running was derived from the text in the 'comments-in-running' descriptions carried in the form book. These descriptions provide details of whether a horse was 'hampered', 'started slowly', 'dwelt in the stalls', 'missed the break', 'finished lame' or 'broke a blood vessel' (not an unusual occurrence in thoroughbred racehorses). My computer was programmed to scan the form book for these descriptions and then to code each of them into a separate variable to be fed into the multiple regression.

In that regression equation I also included a control variable to take account of a horses ability. The simplest way to do this, which takes account of the level of competition in a race, was to use the starting price odds. Thus a horses that went off at long-odds would be expected to have a smaller normalised finishing position than a short priced favourite (remembering that the scale is based between 0.5 to -0.5, with 0.5 being for the best possible finishing position and -0.5 being for the the worst). I was then able to run the analysis to see the independent effect of a horse being hampered, having a poor start etc. on its normalised finishing position.

The results worked out as expected, with bad luck factors reducing the average normalised finishing position by varying degrees. A horse that finished lame was shown to have its normalised finishing position reduced by a massive 0.33. This is hardly surprising because an injured horse is unlikely to perform at its best. However, punters might think that a horse than finished in midfield ran poorly when in actual fact that was a very good performance if account was taken of it's injury.

A horse that broke a blood vessel had its finishing position reduced by 0.004. Again this is not surprising although the effect is fairly small which might be because horses only break blood vessels when they are running flat out, which might mean that they were close to winning or racing to take a hand in the finish when injury struck.

A much bigger negative was whether a horse had a bad start. A bad start reduced the normalised finishing position by 0.1, an effect that might be bigger in sprint races. Horses that were hampered also finished lower down the field than one might have expected had they experienced a clear run. A comment of 'hampered' in the form book means that, on average, a horses normalised finishing position was reduced by 0.06. I also tested various other form book comments but these were not statistically significant predictors of finishing positions.

The next step in my analysis was then to use these estimates for bad luck in running and then to adjust the normalised finishing position to take them into account. This should produce a normalised finishing position that would represent the finishing position that the horse would have achieved had it not experienced what American punters call a 'bad trip'.

The simplest way to adjust form figures for a 'bad trip' is to take a horses normalised finishing position and then to increase it (bigger scores being better) by the amount of compensation that its form comments suggest that it is owned for bad luck in running. The level of compensation is based on our calculated regression weights. Thus a horse that had a normalised finishing position of 0.4, and had started slowly on that run, would have an adjusted normalised finishing position of 0.5 because of the compensation factor for the slow start being 0.1.

The really interesting thing about this process is that if you make these calculations for a horses last race, in all non-handicap flat races, they are shown to be profitable! Indeed if you blindly backed every horse that had a normalised finishing position last time out of zero or greater, after including any compensation that the horse was allowed for bad luck in running, then you would make a profit of 2 per cent on turnover. Okay this is small but this is a really basic strategy. Following this blind strategy would result in you backing a number of horses in the same race, and this would lower returns significantly. However, if you add your own filters to narrow down the number of selections further you should be able to improve significantly on this rate of return.

Does wind surgery improve a horses chance of winning?

New forms of new raw data is slowly emerging to help the British punter. I've discussed the emergence of sectional time data but there is another new form of data that is worth a mention.

A few years ago the BHA required the publication of data on horses that had received a wind operation since their last racecourse appearance. From 19 January 2018 trainers were required to declare if a horse had received surgery for either:

1) Tie back (prosthetic laryngoplasty);

2) Hobday (ventriculography/cordectomy);

3) Epiglottic surgery;

4) Tie forward (dorsal displacement soft palate surgery);

5) Soft palate cautery.

I can't pretend to understand the difference between these forms of surgery but it was a welcome initiative by the British Horse racing Authority to ensure that punters received information on horses that had been operated on for breathing problems.

The issue of a horses ability to breath when under the stress of racing is clearly very important. Some horses, particularly bigger horses, suffer from a difficulty with their breathing when under significant pressure from exercise. Basically in these animal there is a temporary movement of a piece of fleshy tissue into an area through which oxygen flows. This restricts the amount of air a horse can breathe in during a race, especially at the finish when the horse is asked for maximum effort. Those horses that have a breathing problem tend to tire rapidly simply because they are not getting enough oxygen into their bodies to ensure that their muscles are working to maximum effect. Surgery can correct these issues.

Punters need to know which horses have had an operation because it might mean that the horses previous form can be ignored and the horse might be expected to improve as a result of the surgery. However, the question for punters is whether or not horses that have had wind surgery will improve significantly, a little bit or not at all. Once punters understand the impact of wind surgery they can build it into their calculations.

Unfortunately the declaration of wind operations hasn't been around that long and only around five per cent of runners have a wind operation. Therefore the data is a bit thin to make too many conclusions. However, I've been collecting data on horses that have had wind operations since the start of this year and I'm not starting to understand what this data means.

The first thing to say is that my statistics show that at face value wind operations do not seem to improve a horse. The win rate of horses racing in Great Britain that are racing for the first time after a wind operation is around 6.5 per cent, which is lower than the 7 per cent recorded by all other horses. This analysis is based on all jump and flat races run in Great Britain in 2019, and could be misleading as horses with wind problems might be inferior to horses generally and might therefore be expected to have a lower wins to runs ratio than all other horses. There might also be a difference between the impact of wind operations on horses running on the flat and those running in jump races. The theory would be that horses in jump races are under more stress than flat horses and therefore might benefit more from a wind operation than their flat counterparts.

When I divide up my data between flat and jump races I get a completely different set of results. The win rate of wind-op horses over the jumps is 8 per cent compared to 6.9 for all other jump horses. In other words the wind operations seems to have some benefit. In comparison horses that have a wind operation on the flat win at a rate of just 4 per cent and other flat horses win at a rate of 7 per cent. This is big news for punters because it looks as though horses that have a wind operation and are racing over the jumps might be getting some benefit but on the flat a wind operation signals that the horse is less likely to win than the average runner. The reasons for this are not clear but any horse that has had a wind operation and is running on the flat might have a more significant breathing problem and one that is not as easily remedied by the surgery.

The evidence though is still not strong enough to say whether or not wind operations increase or decrease a horses probability of winning. A more sophisticated approach would be try to use a statistical technique called logistic regression to control for differences in the ability of horses and use that method to tell us whether a wind operation increases or decreases a horses probability of winning after controlling for prior ability (as measured by the Racing Post pre-race Master Rating) and field size, as the probability of a horse winning will decrease depending on the number of rivals.

In jump races the statistical analysis is clear enough. The Racing Post Master rating and the number of runners in the race were both big predictors of a horses chances. The presence of a recent wind operation seemed to improve the horses chance of winning, after controlling for prior ability and the number of runners, but the effect was statistically insignificant. In other words the impact of the wind operation appeared positive but could just be a chance finding.

In flat racing the effect of wind operations was negative. The finding was also outside of statistical significance and might still be the result of chance.

What conclusions can be drawn from this analysis? The declaration of horses running for the first time since a wind operation is a fairly recent development. This means that the amount of data is fairly limited and it is probably too early to tell whether horses that have had a wind operation are more likely to win as a result. My analysis suggests that horses over the jumps might benefit from wind operations. However, the effects are not large after taking into account horses prior ability ratings and look to be statistically insignificant. My advice would not to up rate a horses chance as a result of wind operation. The effect of the jockey, trainer, and prior ability of the horse are probably more important factors.

2 THE JOCKEY

Have standards of jockeyship improved since the turn of the century? After watching one of my bets go down due to pilot error I sometimes have my doubts! There is a plenty of serious research on this topic. Scientific research has shown that the biggest improvement in jockeyship in Great Britain occurred between the end of the 19th century and the beginning of the twenty century when the great Todd Sloan came to England and pioneered the crouched riding style that remains to this day. At the time he was laughed at by fellow jockeys, trainers and racegoers but he soon had the last laugh as he was able to get his mounts to run faster and massively improved the chances of the horses that he rode. The scientist have proven that this change in riding style increased horses speeds by around seven per cent.

A recent scientific study has explained why Todd Sloan was so successful. Scientists have shown that when animals carry loads, there is a proportionate increase in energy but this can be reduced if the jockey can pivot themselves in a certain position as the horse moves forward. This would be difficult or impossible with a seated or upright, straight-legged posture – such as the riding style of the 19th century champion jockey Fred Archer. This posture requires substantial work by jockeys, and studies show that successful jockeys need to be extremely fit to maintain the optimum position on a racehorse.

In the twenty-first century there has also been a definite improvement in jockeyship. The scientist have shown that the physical fitness of the jockey is key, and jockey's today are so much fitter and more professional in comparison to the jockeys of just a few decades ago. Indeed as recently as the 1980s I recall stories about jockey's being absolutely plastered from a night out on the town the day before racing, and even stories of the clerk of the scales giving jockey's a bottle of whisky to share to warm them up before racing in the winter over jumps. I'm also certain, although I haven't compiled any statistics on this, that you see far fewer foul-ups by jockeys today than in the past. In the 1970s and 1980s you would see races over the jumps when a jockey would ride a finish a circuit too early, unseat at the slightest interference or stop riding before passing the finishing post. These things still happen but now they make headlines in the racing press whereas in the past these 'pilot errors' seldom got a mention.

The problem for the punter is that the improvements in jockeyship have narrowed the difference between the best and the worst jockeys. In the 1980s and even in the 1990s you could quickly work out which jockeys couldn't even ride a bike. These days it is harder to spot the jockey that can improve a horse or is least likely to unseat. The modern backer therefore needs to use more sophisticated statistics in order to identify subtle differences in jockey ability.

Assessing a jockey's ability

The basic statistics such as number of races victories, number of rides, and the percentage of races won are all interesting but they fail to deal with the main problem with analysing a jockey's performance from the raw statistics, namely that you can't differentiate the best jockey from the best horse. In other words does one jockey look from the statistics to be the more able because he won more races than another jockey, or was it just that he or she was simply riding better quality horses?

I've been applying some statistical techniques to answer this question. The basic idea of my method is to calculate the expected finishing position of a horse from all aspects of it's form, apart from any variable relating to the jockey. My statistical model only considers handicap races, which theoretically should work to equalise the chances of each and every horse in the race. It then takes into account the horses handicap weight, official handicap rating, strike rate of the trainer, previous finishing positions, age of the horse, whether it has previously won over the distance, whether it has previously won over the course, and whether it has previously won on the going. I didn't include the horses starting price, despite it being a good predictor of a horses finishing position, because it has a bias in that popular (possibly more able) jockey's tend to attract the most bets.

Another important point is that my model predicts the normalised finishing position i.e. a horses finishing position relative to the number of runners in the race. This works as follows: a horse that finished 5th of 10 runners ran in midfield and therefore scores 0, but if the horse won it would score 0.5 and if it finished last it would score -0.5. If a horse failed to finish for whatever reason it gets a score of 0.

Once I had created my model I then calculated for each and every handicap race in a ten-year period the expected finishing position of each horse. I then assessed this against the horses actual finishing position. Therefore if a horse was expected to have a normalised finishing position of 0.3 but actually finished better than that and earned a normalised finishing position of 0.4 it showed a difference of 0.1 between it's expected and actual finishing position (i.e. it did better than expected). A good part of this difference might be due to the accuracy of the model and random fluctuations. However, when calculated over hundreds of races the idea would be that these issues are cancelled out and we get some idea about what difference a jockey is contributing to a horses performance (that being the bit not included in the predicted/expected finishing position).

What do the results of this analysis show? These are set out in the Table below for the jockeys that clocked up more than 1,000 rides in the sample period. The data is ranked according to the difference between the actual and expected finishing position.

I chose a sample that was based over the last few seasons when Tony McCoy and Ruby Walsh were both still riding to see if my method could determine who was the better rider. As you can see Ruby Walsh tops the rankings. He makes a positive difference to a horses expected finishing position, with a value of +0.0771. This doesn't sound much, which is a story in itself about the overall contribution of a jockey to a horses chance of winning, but it could make the difference between winning and losing in a tightly competitive race.

The model and overall method looks to be producing a sensible result in that Walsh and McCoy top the Table, although there is a fair gap between the two top riders. In reality I doubt the gap between them was as big as that but it is a result that makes you think.

I have a slight worry that the model has a bias towards riders that ride for only a limited number of top trainers, such as having a retainer to Paul Nichols or Willie Mullins as was the case with Ruby Walsh. The model doesn't take this into account (although I have tried to capture this in the model by including the trainers winners to runners strike rate). It may be the case that the ability of the trainer is exerting more of an influence over the jockey ratings than one would like. In other words it is the ability of the trainer that is making the difference to the horses actual finishing position over the expected position rather than just the jockey. It is hard to get around this and no method of assessing a jockey's ability is going to be able to isolate the sole influence of the jockey over all other factors. However, I think I've got a fairly good method that works better than just the raw statistics.

Mean difference in actual and expected finishing position, by jockey, Great Britain and Ireland

Jockey	Mean diff in actual – expected finish position
R Walsh	.0771
A P McCoy	.0438
Aidan Coleman	.0403
Wayne Hutchinson	.0350
Davy Russell	.0341

Jockey	**Mean diff in actual – expected finish position**
Graham Lee	.0313
Paddy Brennan	.0305
Daryl Jacob	.0288
Richard Johnson	.0246
Barry Fenton	.0244
Jason Maguire	.0241
Noel Fehily	.0237
Tom O'Brien	.0234
P A Carberry	.0225
Barry Geraghty	.0210
Robert Thornton	.0179
Timmy Murphy	.0166
Robert Walford	.0165
Tony Dobbin	.0154
Dominic Elsworth	.0149
Sam Twiston-Davies	.0146
Mark Walsh	.0144

Jockey	Mean diff in actual – expected finish position
P W Flood	.0129
P Carberry	.0126
Nick Scholfield	.0122
D J Casey	.0111

I notice from the Table that Aidan Coleman looks to be a very good jockey. I think many others would share that opinion. Richard Johnson rates the ninth best jockey. He is looking likely to be champion jockey for the next few years and his rating might raise a few eyebrows for not being higher. I personally think he is fantastic and gets the best out of a horse. I'm certainly not saying that my model is perfect, but while the actual rankings may be imperfect the list of jockey's in the top 25 look like the best of the bunch to me.

Not shown are the hundreds of jockey's that look to worsen a horses finishing position! To be honest you don't see too many household names down the bottom of my list, and one would have to conclude that the market for jockey's works fairly well in that the best riders get the best mounts and the most rides and winners. However, Andrew Lynch won't be too pleased. He gets plenty of high profile rides and gets plenty of winners but my analysis would show he isn't adding much over and above the average jockey. I personally think he rides well but my data would suggest otherwise.

I guess even with the best data and analysis racing is all about opinions and you have to take your own view about a jockey. I loved McCoy and I would argue to say that he was the best jockey I've seen but I hope this research, while not ending the arguments, has given you food for thought about how to statistically assess jockey ability.

Can the jockey stay on the horse?

A lot of people (myself included) have done a lot of research on jockeys, and I know a lot of punters blindly follow certain jockeys. Unless you had a decent accumulator bet on Frankie Dettori's 25,000 to 1 'magnificent seven' at Ascot in 1996 then I'm not sure this is a profitable strategy in the long-run. However, the ability of the jockey is clearly very important. The problem is that identifying a good from a bad jockey is that it is fairly hard to come up with one statistic that tell you what you need to know. The number of winners and a jockey's win strike rate is useful but that won't necessarily pick up the rising stars of the future or those jockeys that are simply underrated by trainers and don't get the decent rides that they deserve.

In all the research I have done – and some of it got fairly complex – there is one simple metric that seems to be a good discriminator of jockey ability. The statistic that seems to be matter, from a winner finding point of view, is the ability of a jockey in National Hunt racing to be able to stay in the saddle! Basically jockey's that regularly unseat are bad bets. They might be riding the favourite but if they have a habit of falling off then you need to know this before placing a bet.

You can't find statistics on the subject of unseated rides from the usual sources such as the Racing Post website. There is plenty of data about wins and rides over hurdles and fences, prize money won and the number of place finishes, and even minimum riding weight over the last twelve months, but nothing on how good a jockey was at actually staying on his mount. Of course this is a good thing for those prepared to bother with compiling their own statistics because it is a little bit of information that isn't readily available to other punters and layers and therefore might not be reflected in the horses odds, giving a bit of value to those with the extra bit of data.

Each year I've therefore compiled a fresh set of statistics on jockeys that unseat and publish them on www.profitablebetting.co.uk.

The first thing to note is the definition of an 'unseat' and how it differs from a fall in the form book. Professional race readers, who compile the official form book, determine whether a horse has fallen or if the jockey fell off. A fall is basically when the jockey had no chance of staying on board because the horse physically hit the deck. An unseat is when the horse might have made a mistake jumping a fence but remained on its feet but the jockey was unable to remain in the saddle. In practice there is quite a wide range of unseats. There are plenty of occasions when the horse has made such an error that no jockey, unless super glued to the saddle, is going to be able to keep the partnership intact. However, there are also plenty of occasions when you think that a jockey simply fell off when another jockey might have been able to stay in the saddle.

I've analysed the results of all jump races run in Great Britain and Ireland in 2019. For reasons of space, and to cut out the noise from small numbers, I've restricted the results to jockeys that had one hundred rides or more over the period. I haven't distinguished between hurdle and chase races to keep the sample as large as possible. The results are set out in the Table below.

The Table doesn't make good reading for Paddy Kennedy, Bryan Carver, Charlie Price, Hugh Morgan, Dave Crosse, Paul O'Brien, Brendan Powell, James O'Sullivan, Jody McGarvey, David Mullins, Connor Brace, Ricky Doyle and Craig Nichol. They all fall off more than 3 times in every hundred rides. Brendan Powell also deserves a special mention because he featured near the top of my 2018 statistics. At least he is consistent!

Overall the whole group of jockeys that had more than 100 rides in 2019 recorded 36803 rides between them and 513 unseats. This means that on average a jockey can expect to unseat 1.39 times per 100 rides. As you would expect big name jockeys fall off at less than the average. Richard Johnson and Sam Twiston-Davies have lots of rides but record very few unseats.

However, there are a group of riders that have plenty of rides (more than 200 rides in 2019) but have an unseat rate of 0.5% or less. The names I would pick out would be Darragh O'Keeffe, Sean Quinlan, Gavin Sheehan, William Kennedy, Alain Cawley, Aidan Coleman, Denis O'Regan, Danny Mullins, Sean Flanagan, Harry Skelton, Bryony Frost, Paddy Brennan, Harry Cobden, and James Davies. Among this select band are several jockeys that consistently record very few unseats.

I would give a special mention to Davy Russell, Denis O'Regan, Sean Quinlan, Harry Skelton, and Paddy Brennan because they also recorded very few unseats in 2018 as well.

A gold star must go to Davy Russell. He is one of my favourite jockeys and he seems to get good priced winners and always records a low proportion of unseats. Every year I compile these figures and he features near the bottom every time. A superb horseman.

There are some jockeys that have more than 100 rides but don't seem to have recorded any unseats in my database. I need to check for errors but even allowing for the odd one or two missed unseats James Davies, A P Heskin, Conor Maxwell, Marc Goldstein, Kevin Jones, Cathal Landers, Tabitha Worsley, Jordan Nailor, Fergus Gregory, David England, and Conor Ring are clearly excellent National Hunt jockeys. The full list of jockey statistics are available from www.profitablebetting.co.uk.

Unseated rider statistics for jump jockeys in 2019, Great Britain and Ireland

Jockey	Rides	Unseats	% Unseat
Paddy Kennedy	149	8	5.37%
Bryan Carver	121	5	4.13%
Charlie Price	124	5	4.03%
Hugh Morgan	149	6	4.03%
Dave Crosse	110	4	3.64%
Paul O'Brien	144	5	3.47%
Brendan Powell	233	8	3.43%

Jockey	Rides	Unseats	% Unseat
James O'Sullivan	147	5	3.40%
Jody McGarvey	207	7	3.38%
David Mullins	193	6	3.11%
Connor Brace	290	9	3.10%
Ricky Doyle	290	9	3.10%
Craig Nichol	196	6	3.06%
Trevor Ryan	101	3	2.97%
Lorcan Murtagh	135	4	2.96%
Ambrose McCurtin	137	4	2.92%
Callum Bewley	209	6	2.87%
Mark Enright	140	4	2.86%
Liam Treadwell	106	3	2.83%
B J Cooper	180	5	2.78%
L P Dempsey	332	9	2.71%
Joshua Moore	227	6	2.64%
Barry Browne	115	3	2.61%
Sean Houlihan	235	6	2.55%
Harry Reed	159	4	2.52%
Niall P Madden	160	4	2.50%

Jockey	Rides	Unseats	% Unseat
Sean Bowen	532	13	2.44%
David Noonan	370	9	2.43%
Kevin Brouder	247	6	2.43%
Robbie Power	401	9	2.24%
Sam Coltherd	225	5	2.22%
Ross Chapman	271	6	2.21%
Henry Brooke	408	9	2.21%
Charlie Deutsch	229	5	2.18%
Jamie Moore	413	9	2.18%
Donal McInerney	235	5	2.13%
Phillip Enright	479	10	2.09%
Stephen Mulqueen	145	3	2.07%
Mikey Hamill	146	3	2.05%
Micheal Nolan	195	4	2.05%
Jonathan Moore	347	7	2.02%
Conor McNamara	201	4	1.99%
Jonjo O'Neill Jr	356	7	1.97%
Jack Kennedy	365	7	1.92%

Jockey	Rides	Unseats	% Unseat
Charlie Todd	159	3	1.89%
Tom Bellamy	213	4	1.88%
Liam Gilligan	108	2	1.85%
Tom Cannon	382	7	1.83%
Brian Hayes	280	5	1.79%
Thomas Willmott	113	2	1.77%
Tom O'Brien	455	8	1.76%
Page Fuller	232	4	1.72%
Jack Quinlan	234	4	1.71%
Ryan Day	118	2	1.69%
Donagh Meyler	296	5	1.69%
Shane Shortall	119	2	1.68%
Keith Donoghue	180	3	1.67%
Rex Dingle	186	3	1.61%
Rachael Blackmore	559	9	1.61%
J J Slevin	383	6	1.57%
Robert Dunne	257	4	1.56%
Stan Sheppard	130	2	1.54%

Jockey	Rides	Unseats	% Unseat
D G Hogan	133	2	1.50%
Ben Poste	274	4	1.46%
Lorcan Williams	138	2	1.45%
Katie O'Farrell	140	2	1.43%
Leighton Aspell	429	6	1.40%
Harry Bannister	215	3	1.40%
Wayne Hutchinson	215	3	1.40%
Richard Patrick	216	3	1.39%
Charlie Hammond	218	3	1.38%
James Best	367	5	1.36%
Kielan Woods	295	4	1.36%
Jamie Bargary	150	2	1.33%
Liam Quinlan	152	2	1.32%
Conor O'Farrell	230	3	1.30%
Jeremiah McGrath	233	3	1.29%
Jonathan Burke	389	5	1.29%
Tom Scudamore	545	7	1.28%
Adam Short	397	5	1.26%

Jockey	Rides	Unseats	% Unseat
Ben Jones	159	2	1.26%
Blair Campbell	160	2	1.25%
Thomas Dowson	246	3	1.22%
Ciaran Gethings	250	3	1.20%
Conor Orr	181	2	1.10%
Richard Johnson	843	9	1.07%
Derek Fox	191	2	1.05%
David Bass	294	3	1.02%
James Bowen	399	4	1.00%
Edward Austin	100	1	1.00%
Jamie Hamilton	203	2	0.99%
Davy Russell	411	4	0.97%
Mark Walsh	319	3	0.94%
Alan Johns	323	3	0.93%
Ryan Treacy	216	2	0.93%
Adam Wedge	454	4	0.88%
Kevin Sexton	118	1	0.85%
Simon Torrens	118	1	0.85%

Jockey	Rides	Unseats	% Unseat
Jonathan England	119	1	0.84%
Brian Hughes	730	6	0.82%
Danny McMenamin	258	2	0.78%
Nico de Boinville	397	3	0.76%
Billy Garritty	136	1	0.74%
Sam Twiston-Davies	694	5	0.72%
Lucy Alexander	142	1	0.70%
Max Kendrick	145	1	0.69%
Paul Townend	446	3	0.67%
Andrew Ring	149	1	0.67%
Sean O'Keeffe	308	2	0.65%
Danny Cook	310	2	0.65%
Daryl Jacob	317	2	0.63%
Barry Geraghty	159	1	0.63%
Patrick Corbett	165	1	0.61%
Bridget Andrews	168	1	0.60%
Richie McLernon	347	2	0.58%
Nick Scholfield	369	2	0.54%

Jockey	Rides	Unseats	% Unseat
Lee Edwards	196	1	0.51%
Darragh O'Keeffe	400	2	0.50%
Sean Quinlan	406	2	0.49%
Gavin Sheehan	424	2	0.47%
William Kennedy	233	1	0.43%
Alain Cawley	241	1	0.41%
Aidan Coleman	489	2	0.41%
Denis O'Regan	253	1	0.40%
Danny Mullins	508	2	0.39%
Sean Flanagan	586	2	0.34%
Harry Skelton	594	2	0.34%
Bryony Frost	339	1	0.29%
Paddy Brennan	456	1	0.22%
Harry Cobden	507	1	0.20%
James Davies	241	0	0.00%
A P Heskin	176	0	0.00%
Conor Maxwell	163	0	0.00%
Marc Goldstein	143	0	0.00%

Jockey	**Rides**	**Unseats**	**% Unseat**
Kevin Jones	135	0	0.00%
Cathal Landers	130	0	0.00%
Tabitha Worsley	128	0	0.00%
Jordan Nailor	110	0	0.00%
Fergus Gregory	104	0	0.00%
David England	102	0	0.00%
Conor Ring	101	0	0.00%

3 THE OWNER, BREEDER AND THE TRAINER

Someone once said that to make a fortune from owning racehorses you had to start with a bigger one. Owning a racehorse is certainly an expensive business, and, as with the rest of life, there is a gigantic gulf between the richest owners at the top and the rest.

Those owners at the top of the tree, such as Sheikh Mohammed and Coolmore, have the financial power to employ the best trainers, provide the best training facilities and utilise the latest advances in science and technology to give them an edge. This is more true today than in the past because the use of science and technology in horse racing has rapidly accelerated this century.

The richest owners have equipped their trainers with artificial-surface gallops, equine spas and provided them with access to the best in veterinary medicine. The best trainers are now able to take the guesswork out of training by employing science to get and keep their horses fit. For example, wind operations used to be based on guesswork but now trainers can put an endoscope in a horse whilst it is galloping and the data is transmitted back to a computer for analysis to see if the horse has a problem and what type of operation will be the most effective in terms of increasing the horses performance. Similarly with lameness, swelling, muscular and skeletal problems horses can now have regular MRI scans to predict and prevent injury before it occurs by resting them before a problem occurs.

There is also device available called a 'smart saddle', which has a sensor embedded within it that records data about a horse's gait, stride, symmetry, acceleration and jumping ability. This and other devices can help a trainer to tailor a training regime to that specific horse's needs.

The breeding of racehorses is also getting more precise. The traditional breeder would make a decision of which horses to mate by a study of their pedigrees, but pedigree can be a poor guide to quality: an ancestor five generations back contributes just three per cent of an animal's DNA. Indeed there are many examples of terrible purchases at the sales.

The Green Monkey had an impeccable pedigree and sold at auction for $16m – the highest price of a publicly auctioned thoroughbred. It ran just four times and failed to win once. However, The Green Monkey looks cheap when compared to Snaafi Dancer, who cost Sheikh Mohammed $10m in the early 1980s (roughly $20m in today's money). The horse was sent into training with John Dunlop but never raced. It was reported that he was so slow in training that it would have been embarrassing to run him in public. All though was not lost. His Northern Dancer pedigree might still mean that he could be a decent stallion. Unfortunately when he was retired to stud he was discovered to have fertility problems. Breeding racehorses can make a fool of even the richest and most powerful owners on the planet.

The traditional methods of breeding horses from a study of pedigrees is now giving way to science. There are now companies that offer DNA screening for racehorse performance. They are now using genome analysis from thousands of animals to identify markers linked to equine stamina and strength. These test are also used to determine whether a horse is best suited to be a sprinter, a long-distance stayer or a middle-distance performer.

What does all this mean for the punter in the twenty-first century? It might all seem irrelevant when considering the form of the runners for the three o'clock at Newmarket but it actual fact these developments will work to create a bigger divide between the horses that have the right connections and the rest. It will be the richest and most powerful owners, trainers and breeders that can employ these scientific and technological developments to give them an edge over the competition. The lesson for the punter is to identify and stay on the side of the biggest owners and the best trainers, and know when they are in form.

Is the trainer in-form?

You can spend hours studying the form of each horse in a race. After all your careful study you might have narrowed down the field of a competitive handicap to a few live contenders, and may be thinking of your final bets. You then notice that your favoured selection is trained by someone who hasn't had a winner in ages and the stable in badly out of form. Do you stick with your selection or opt for the next best horse in the race, who looks to have a bit to find on your main selection, but is trained by someone who is on hot streak? Does the form of the stable matter that much?

The answer to that last question is easy. Stables that are out-of-form simply don't make for good betting propositions. The horses in the stable might be blue blooded classic horses that would normally be far to good for their opponents, but if the stable hasn't had a winner for several weeks then you should keep your cash in your wallet.

Racing stables are a bit like primary schools. They are basically germ factories, and even with a strict hygiene regime one horse will inevitably pick up an infection from another horse while at the races. The infection will then spread across the yard and infect all the other horses. Unfortunately it might take a time to realise that the horses are under the weather, with the problem only be suspected after a number of the horses under perform on the track. This can be costly to any punter that hasn't considered the recent form of the trainer.

The loss of form can also have a psychological impact on a stable, and one that can last beyond the period of the infection. The trainer might start to question their methods, and stable staff might also lose confidence. All of this could mean that things get changed around when they don't need to, and bad decisions get made which in turn impact on the stables performance. The form of a stable is therefore important but it is sometimes hard to tell when a stable in going in and out of form.

There are two main methods for assessing a stable that is either in or out of form. The most simple is to look at the winners to runners ratio of a trainer over a period of 14 days. This seems to provide an important clue as to whether a stable is suffering from some virus because if the winners dry up then you know that the stable is possibly suffering from some dreaded virus.

The weakness of the crude, rolling 14 day statistics is that they don't provide a comparative estimate of what the trainers winners to runners ratio should be given the quality of the horses that they have in their care. For example, if a trainer has a stable full of useless horses then they aren't going to get any winners in fourteen days or in a thousand days! The Racing Post have come up with a statistics that provides a more sophisticated method for assessing trainer form. This is the "Ran To Form" statistic or RTF%, as it is depicted in the Racing Post racecards.

The Racing Post explains that RTF% is the percentage of a trainer's horses who have 'run to form' in the last 14 days. This means that if a trainer runs 100 horses in 14 days and 50 of them ran to form then the RTF% would be 50%. The method the Racing Post uses to assess whether a horse has ran to form is to take the horses Racing Post Master Rating (the newspapers own handicap rating for a horse, which should indicate its ability) and then to measure whether the horse ran close to that rating in the race that it contested. Therefore if a horse was rated 100 before the race but finished tailed off it might earn a Racing Post Rating of 50 for that performance. This is clearly a very poor run and the horse wouldn't be said to have ran to the form it was (in theory) capable of producing. Over a number of runners if a trainer is having a lot of horses under performing on this measure then they will record a low RTF statistic.

I've read in a few places that the RTF statistic sounds a good one to use in theory but is hopeless in practice. This assessment is based on the fact that you can find plenty of losers that are trained by trainers that record an RTF statistic of 100%. However, I've seen no statistical evidence on the performance of the RTF measure, and haven't seen any data on how it compares to the simple two week winners to runners strike rate measure. To put this right I've analysed the data on both metrics. The data on the RTF measure is recorded in the Table below.

Ran to form % bands, and winners to runners strike rate

	Wins	Runs	Win %
RTF <10%	417	6,974	6.0%
>10% <20%	87	1,400	6.2%
>20% <30%	337	4,307	7.8%
>30% <40%	617	7,021	8.8%
>40% <50%	1,092	10,308	10.6%
>50% <60%	1,805	15,028	12.0%
>60% <70%	1,143	8,291	13.8%
>70% <80%	486	3,020	16.1%
>80% <90%	135	1,038	13.0%
>90%	151	1,870	8.1%
All	6,270	59,257	10.6%

Looking at the data in the Table above it is clear that the RTF is a good discriminator of winners, which demonstrates that recent trainer form is an important factor to consider before placing a bet. The overall strike rate of all runners in my sample is 10.6%. However, horses trained by trainers with a RTF statistic of less than 40% win at below the average rate. Indeed the runners of trainers with a RTF below 20% win at a rate of around 6%. In contrast runners of trainers with an RTF of between 70 and 80% win at a rate of over 16%. Curiously trainers with an RTF of more than 80% record a lower strike rate. Indeed those with a RTF of more than 90% win at a rate of just 8 per cent. This I think can be explained by the fact that trainers with very high RTF statistics tend to have only a couple of runners within the two week period. This means that a trainer might have had just two runners that both ran to form in the last fortnight. That would give him or her an RTF of 100% but the sample if just too small to be reliable. The RTF statistic at the high extreme might be biased towards small stables that don't have many runners and who might normally have fairly low strike rates because the horses they train are of low quality.

Overall the RTF seems to do a pretty good job at discriminating between winners and losers based on the recent form of the trainer. One just needs to be cautious about drawing too many conclusions about the form of the trainer if they have had only a small number of runners within the last 14 days.

In the Table below I've tried to show the relationship between a trainers strike rate with their runners over the last 14 days and the likelihood of their next runner winning. Again you can see that trainers with a strike rate of below 10% do very badly with their runners, and these runners win at a rate of just 8.2% whereas the runners of trainers with a strike rate of between 20 and 50% win at a rate of between 15 and 17%. The samples get too small at the high extremes but it is pretty clear that the runners of trainers with a strike rate of more than 20% win at almost twice the rate of those with a strike rate of below 10%.

The win rate of runners according to the strike rate of trainers over a 14 day period

Trainers win rate, last 14 days	Wins	Runs	Win %
<10%	2537	31126	8.2%
>10% <20%	2191	17774	12.3%
>20% <30%	1061	7094	15.0%
>30% <40%	305	1975	15.4%
>40% <50%	72	421	17.1%
>50% <60%	68	564	12.1%
>60% <70%	15	101	14.9%
>70% <80%	2	16	12.5%
>80% <90%	0	3	0.0%
>90%	19	183	10.4%
All	6270	59257	10.6%

In summary, the statistical analysis presented here is pretty clear that recent trainer form is an important factor in deciding on which horse to back. All other things being equal you would be more likely to back a winner by siding with the horse that is trained by a trainer in form. However, this isn't the same as saying that the horse in a race that is trained by the trainer with the best recent record is the one more likely to win. The measures of trainer form aren't that precise and the data at the high extremes seems to get pretty thin, or has significant biases. The metrics look to be better at helping to avoid betting on horses trained by trainers that are badly out of form. For instance, I wouldn't be keen to back a horse trained by someone with an RTF of less than 20%. The runners from these stables might be ill and suffering from some sort of virus. The same would apply to horses trained by trainers that have recorded a strike rate of less than 10% with their runners in the last 14 days.

In terms of which metric might be best this is a hard question and both do the job of identifying trainers that are out of form. The RTF measure though looks to be slightly better at discriminating between trainers level of recent form, provided that you are sceptical about trainers with very high RTF scores.

Can the trainer get a horse fit? The strike rate of National Hunt trainers with horses running after a lay-off.

You can pick plenty of winners by focussing on the horses trained by the best trainers. The rationale is obvious. It is the trainer who selects the races in which a horse will run, chooses the jockey and determines the overall training regime of the horse. It is they who are responsible for getting a horse fit and dealing with its various ailments. The difficulty for punters is working out which are the best trainers.

To some extent market forces will provide important clues as to the ability of different trainers. The best trainers will have the best horses and/or the most number of horses as more owners will be drawn to trainers that get winners, and the richest owners with the best horses will select the trainer that they judge to be the best. However, market forces don't always get it right and statistical analysis can provide objective evidence of trainers that might be better than the market might suggest.

One of the factors that I think can be important for unearthing decent priced winners is the ability of a trainer to get a horse fit after a lay-off. Punters tend to over bet horses with good recent form and tend to downplay the chances of horses that are returning to the track after a lay-off. For example, you might have two horses in a race with identical abilities but one horse raced in the last week and the other horse hadn't raced for 100 days or more. The horse with the recent outing will always be the favourite to beat the horses that is retuning after a break.

There are clearly good reasons for this. A horse with good recent form is clearly in good health whereas the horse that has had a break might have had some problem that has kept it off the track. The ailment might have required box rest and the trainer may have needed plenty of time to get it back to fitness. The question then becomes one of whether the horse is fit enough to win. This is very difficult. In days of old a trainer would determine whether a horse was race fit by looking at it whereas today veterinary science plays a big part. Inevitably some trainers are better than this than others.

I've looked at the results for National Hunt trainers over the last 12 months and calculated the number of runners and the number of winners that each trainer had with horses that had been off the track for 100 days or more. The results are presented in the Table below and are ordered by strike rate.

Table: Trainers strike rate with horses off the track for 100 days+

Trainer	Wins 100day+	Runners 100day+	% Wins 100day+
Nicky Henderson	26	93	28.0%
W P Mullins	28	114	24.6%
Kim Bailey	12	52	23.1%
Dr Richard Newland	9	39	23.1%
Philip Kirby	7	35	20.0%
Tom Lacey	6	32	18.8%
Colin Tizzard	18	98	18.4%
Paul Nicholls	22	120	18.3%
Olly Murphy	13	71	18.3%
Jeremy Scott	6	34	17.6%
Noel Meade	12	69	17.4%
Dan Skelton	28	162	17.3%
Joseph Patrick O'Brien	13	78	16.7%
Ian Williams	8	49	16.3%
Nicky Richards	7	46	15.2%
Nigel Twiston-Davies	15	102	14.7%
Jamie Snowden	6	41	14.6%

Trainer	Wins 100day+	Runners 100day+	% Wins 100day+
Fergal O'Brien	12	85	14.1%
Philip Hobbs	16	115	13.9%
Gary Moore	9	65	13.8%
Gordon Elliott	24	179	13.4%
Lucinda Russell	9	71	12.7%
Ben Pauling	7	56	12.5%
Alan King	9	81	11.1%
Tom George	9	81	11.1%
Oliver Sherwood	5	45	11.1%
Seamus Mullins	5	45	11.1%
Emma Lavelle	6	55	10.9%
Jonjo O'Neill	10	94	10.6%
Harry Fry	5	48	10.4%
Warren Greatrex	6	58	10.3%
Peter Bowen	5	52	9.6%
Venetia Williams	6	63	9.5%
Martin Keighley	3	32	9.4%
Henry De Bromhead	9	99	9.1%

Trainer	**Wins 100day+**	**Runners 100day+**	**% Wins 100day+**
Evan Williams	6	72	8.3%
Brian Ellison	3	40	7.5%
Charlie Longsdon	4	56	7.1%
Tim Vaughan	5	71	7.0%
Micky Hammond	4	57	7.0%
Donald McCain	6	90	6.7%
N W Alexander	3	45	6.7%
Nigel Hawke	2	30	6.7%
Graeme McPherson	2	33	6.1%
Michael Scudamore	2	33	6.1%
Neil Mulholland	5	88	5.7%
Sue Smith	2	37	5.4%
Mrs John Harrington	3	61	4.9%
David Pipe	3	62	4.8%
Rebecca Menzies	1	31	3.2%
S J Mahon	1	31	3.2%
Kerry Lee	1	33	3.0%
A J Martin	1	44	2.3%

Trainer	Wins 100day+	Runners 100day+	% Wins 100day+
Peter Fahey	0	35	0.0%
Denis Gerard Hogan	0	30	0.0%

In terms of methodology the analysis is restricted to trainers that had 30 or more runners in National Hunt races (including National Hunt flat races) that hadn't raced for 100 days or more. This was to provide a sufficient sample and to make the conclusions more reliable. Inevitably this focuses the analysis on those trainers with large numbers of horses. There might be smaller yards that are good at getting a horse fit after a lay-off but they are not included here. However, as they will account for fewer runners overall we aren't losing too much information. The data covers results in Great Britain and Ireland during a 12 month period.

The first thing to note about the statistical table is that when it is ordered by strike rate the two trainers that come out first and second are probably the two trainers that most people would consider to be the best and are probably the two trainers that would come out top on any statistical measure. Indeed Nicky Henderson and Willie Mullins would probably have the richest owners and the best horses of any trainer in the Table. The interesting thing is that they are also clearly the best trainers at getting a horse fit as Nicky Henderson has a strike race with lay-off horses of nearly 28 per cent and Willie Mullins has a strike rate of nearly one winner in every four runners. Indeed some of the trainers listed are probably doing as well with horses racing after a lay-off as they do with all of their runners.

Kim Bailey and Dr Richard Newland are very good trainers and appear near the top of the list. However, they probably don't get the quality of horse that they deserve. A smaller trainer that seems particularly able in getting a horse fit after a lay off if Jeremy Scott. Philip Kirby, Tom Lacy and Olly Murphy also seem to now the time of day when it comes to getting a horse fit. These less well known trainers are the real money spinners as other punters might underrate the chances of their horses, particularly if they have been off the track for a period of time. This though doesn't look to be enough of a barrier for trainers as they record plenty of winners between them with their 'lay-off' horses.

There are some trainers that have a very low strike rate with horses after a lay-off. A trainer with less than a five per cent strike rate with this type of horse might be a cause for concern. I have to say that I was surprised to see David Pipe down the list as the Pipe stable is renowned for getting horses fit and Martin Pipe, father of David, basically pioneered scientific methods for getting a horse to race fitness. The data doesn't lie but it might not be telling the full story. Horses that have been off the track for 100 days or more might be off the track for different reasons. Top class horses, like the ones in the Henderson and Willie Mullins yards, tend not to race that often and the 100 day off horses in their respective samples might be biased towards top class horses that win consistently. This might account for the very high strike rate of Mullins and Henderson with horses that have been off the track for 100 days or more. Other trainers might be working with horses that are off the track because of illness. It will be much harder to win with this type of horse and a five per cent strike rate for this type of horse might actually be very good. Therefore the Table shouldn't necessarily be seen as 100 per cent proof of trainers ability to get a horse fit. However, from a punting perspective this doesn't necessarily matter as you simply want to be siding with horses trained by trainers that have a high winner to runner ratio with horses that have been of the track for a while as other punters tend to downgrade the chances of horses that have been off the track for a long period.

What can we conclude from this analysis? To me it is pretty clear that in National Hunt racing in particular the fitness of the horse has a big influence on results. Some trainers are better at getting a horse fully race fit than others and any analysis that sheds some light on this should be useful for punters. The data has some caveats but generally speaking it looks like you could get an edge by betting on horses that have been off the track for 100 days or more when they are trained by trainers that have a high strike rate with horses racing after a lay-off.

Is JP McManus providing free racing tips?

I haven't seen that much research on the statistical patterns associated with racehorse owners, and I think that this is an area that is overlooked. However, it is a tricky area to research statistically because the details of who owns a horse are often changed, especially if the horse is jointly owned. For example, one owner in the partnership might be the lead name listed one season but then the ownership details are then changed the next season to give the other owner the honour. The horses registered colours might also change as a result. You also have the problem with syndicates that might register a different syndicate name for every horse they own. The only way around these problems is to analyse the records of the major owners that always run their horses under their own name and seldom enter ownership partnerships.

I have spent sometime analysing the record of horses owned by JP McManus. For those who don't know (where have you been?) JP McManus is one of the biggest and most famous race horse owners in the country. His distinctive green-and-gold-hooped racing colours are known to most punters and will forever be associated with the exploits of the legendary Istabraq, a three-time winner of the Champion Hurdle. He has amassed himself a huge fortune as both a bookmaker and punter, and is one of the biggest owners in National Hunt racing.

I'm sure to his closest friends JP McManus gives plenty of sound betting advice but, despite being a generous fellow (he donates large sums to a number of charities) I'm not aware of him giving away any free tips, and I don't think he needs to add to his fortune by setting up a telephone tipping line. However, while watching a race the other day, which included a couple of McManus owned runners, I wondered whether he was inadvertently giving a tip by running one horse in his first colours and the other horse in his second colours. After watching the horse in the McManus first colours win easily I started to think that maybe owners with multiple runners in a race are giving punters inside information by running one runner in their first colours and the lesser fancied runners in their second or third colours. Could owners choice of silks be some sort of semaphore system for picking winners?

I started to test my hypothesis by researching owners and their silks, and their winning strike rates by first and second colours. This research quickly became problematic because of the sheer number of owners and syndicates, and I found it difficult to work out which set of colours were the owners first, second, third, fourth, and fifth colours etc. For example, Gigginstown Stud sometime have several runners in a race and while the first colours and obvious you can't be sure of what colours represent the third and fourth owners choice of silks.

To make things easier I established a simple rule of thumb. The first colours were defined by me as the set of colours that that the owner used most often over a number of seasons, and the second and third colours etc. were assigned according to the frequency in which they were used. This classification wasn't simple because on occasion an owner might change their racing colours, but it seemed to work well enough.

A bigger problem for working out an owners first choice of silks was that different information sources sometimes described an owners colours differently. For example, in one publication I found that the McManus silks were sometimes described as "green-and-gold-hooped" but sometimes as "green-and-orange-hooped". This isn't a problem when considering the major owners as their first colours are well-known but for the smaller owners it is harder to recognise. The differences between the reporting of colours in the racing press might lead to a few errors in my analysis but I hoped that over a large enough sample these errors would wash out.

In my analysis I've also focussed on jump racing because you seem to get more runners in the same ownership under that code, although that isn't the case in Ireland where you have the Coolmore boys dominating. However, it is hard to work out which horse is running in the first colours because the Coolmore owners Magnier, Tabor, and Smith often split ownership between them and therefore they could run three horses in a race but each horse would run in the first colours of each Coolmore owner, yet basically the syndicate has three runners in the race.

Once I'd assembled my data the first thing I did was pull out all the races that had runners owned by the same owner. This gave me around 8,600 races. As you would expect these were mostly large field affairs. I then put a flag on the data to denote whether the horse that was running in the owners first colours and then put another flag on horse or horses running in the owners other colours. I could have divided the data into horses wearing the second, third or fourth colours etc. but this wasn't that useful as the sample sizes get very small.

When I ran the analysis I got the finding that I probably expected. Horses running in an owners first colours won at a rate of 8.2 per cent whereas the horses running in the owners other colours won at a rate of 6.2 per cent. In other words the horse in the owners first colours is 1.3 times more likely to win than the owners other runners. Therefore, before considering any other factor, the colours of the owners silks seem to predict winners. I personally haven't seen this point statistically proven before.

However, my next thought was that it would be hard to profit from this information because basically most punters and newspaper pundits will take some account of this information, even if they don't have access to the statistics to quantify its precise relevance. I therefore looked at the profitability of betting blindly on owners first colours in races where an owner had more than one runner in a race. Unfortunately, you would lose a heap of cash betting on these runners blindly. The rate of loss would be about 48p for every pound staked at the Betfair starting price. Ouch! You would do a bit better by actually betting the owners other runners. In following that strategy you would lose only around 34p in every pound staked.

This though got me thinking. Maybe the strategy should be to back the owners second string. They might represent good value as punters might be put off by the fact that they are racing in the owners second colours. This strategy though would need to cut out complete no hopers. We wouldn't want to be betting on pacemakers for more fancied runners. We would need to see a bit of confidence behind the second string. My strategy was therefore to simply bet the owners second string when they were less than 5 to 1 on their opening show with the bookmakers. This should cut out the no hopers. Some cynics might also argue that this might also pick up the second string runners that might actually be more fancied but the owner is trying to put off punters and get better odds by running the horse in his or her second colours!

The results of this analysis show a big turnaround. Backing an owners second string when starting at less than 5 to 1 on the first show would yield a 17 per cent profit on turnover! Unfortunately you are never going to get that rich following this simple system because you don't get huge numbers of races when an owner has more than one runner in a race. However, the analysis shows that you shouldn't be put off backing an owners second string.

Sire analysis

As mentioned earlier, breeding practices often change and the sire can exert a major influence on some races, particularly in sprints of six furlongs and less. In these races you you need a horse that is bred for speed. However, knowledge of sire characteristics is really only profitable when a horse is doing something that it has never done before. When a horse has ran a few times then you can work out a horses preference for distance, going etc from it's past performance data. Sire analysis is therefore very useful when horses debut on the all-weather as some horses either like the surface or not, or when they are making a debut in a sprint.

I've done some analysis on the win strike rate of sires on the all-weather in sprint races as an example of how useful sire analysis can be. The data is presented in the Table below. The analysis to restricted to sires that had at least 50 runners over the last three years in all-weather sprint races.

Table: Strike rate of sires in all-weather sprint races

Sire	Wins	Runs	% Win
Dark Angel	53	263	20.0%
Shamardal	23	116	20.0%
Baltic King	10	54	19.0%
War Front	10	52	19.0%
Bated Breath	30	168	18.0%
Rock Of Gibraltar	9	51	18.0%
Footstepsinthesand	22	128	17.0%
Orientor	10	60	17.0%
Oasis Dream	27	166	16.0%
Mayson	20	126	16.0%
Dragon Pulse	17	105	16.0%

Sire	**Wins**	**Runs**	**% Win**
Delegator	13	79	16.0%
Raven's Pass	12	73	16.0%
Frozen Power	9	55	16.0%
Dandy Man	51	339	15.0%
Showcasing	33	220	15.0%
Lilbourne Lad	13	85	15.0%
Aqlaam	9	61	15.0%
Kyllachy	61	434	14.0%
Invincible Spirit	43	307	14.0%
Canford Cliffs	14	99	14.0%
Red Clubs	10	73	14.0%
Choisir	10	70	14.0%
Red Jazz	7	51	14.0%
Sayif	7	50	14.0%
Kodiac	85	655	13.0%
Exceed And Excel	58	445	13.0%
Clodovil	16	121	13.0%
Sepoy	16	120	13.0%

Sire	Wins	Runs	% Win
Paco Boy	14	111	13.0%
Sir Prancealot	18	154	12.0%
Acclamation	54	447	12.0%
Dream Ahead	17	139	12.0%
Pivotal	14	114	12.0%
Avonbridge	13	105	12.0%
Iffraaj	11	94	12.0%
Lethal Force	17	141	12.0%
Zebedee	41	376	11.0%
Society Rock	24	216	11.0%
Sakhee's Secret	14	126	11.0%
Harbour Watch	12	105	11.0%
Sleeping Indian	11	104	11.0%
Intense Focus	9	84	11.0%
Major Cadeaux	7	66	11.0%
Lawman	7	65	11.0%
Lope De Vega	7	62	11.0%
Byron	6	54	11.0%

Sire	Wins	Runs	% Win
Assertive	11	98	11.0%
Camacho	22	222	10.0%
Pastoral Pursuits	25	252	10.0%
Poet's Voice	21	206	10.0%
Swiss Spirit	19	191	10.0%
Bahamian Bounty	18	178	10.0%
Dutch Art	18	178	10.0%
Approve	14	139	10.0%
Foxwedge	12	124	10.0%
Helmet	7	69	10.0%
Elnadim	7	68	10.0%
Kheleyf	29	318	9.0%
Piccolo	28	314	9.0%
Royal Applause	17	185	9.0%
Zoffany	7	80	9.0%
Excelebration	5	58	9.0%
Heeraat	5	55	9.0%
Captain Gerrard	20	253	8.0%

Sire	**Wins**	**Runs**	**% Win**
Compton Place	18	229	8.0%
Holy Roman Emperor	9	111	8.0%
Multiplex	7	87	8.0%
Stimulation	6	75	8.0%
Arcano	7	107	7.0%
Hellvelyn	6	84	7.0%
Havana Gold	6	82	7.0%
Epaulette	5	75	7.0%
Equiano	24	401	6.0%
Monsieur Bond	14	239	6.0%
Street Cry	3	54	6.0%
Power	3	50	6.0%
Coach House	4	67	6.0%
Fast Company	6	112	5.0%
Casamento	3	75	4.0%
Firebreak	2	55	4.0%
Tagula	2	64	3.0%
Requinto	2	62	3.0%

Sire	Wins	Runs	% Win
Majestic Missile	2	58	3.0%
Captain Rio	1	58	2.0%
Bushranger	1	72	1.0%

You will have noticed the huge range in strike rates between the sires. For example, Dark Angel has a strike rate of 20 per cent in all-weather sprints but Bushranger had 72 runners but only one winner. Therefore you would be crazy to back a horse sired by Bushranger when making it's debut in an all-weather sprint but a horse sired by Dark Angel would be of definite interest.

Some horses perform better on different types of going. On the all-weather the fibresand surface at Southwell is very different to the other all-weather surfaces used at the other all-weather tracks. This often catches out the unwary because a horse that has shown good form on the all-weather at Wolverhampton might under perform at Southwell on its slower surface. A clue as to how a horse might perform when making its debut at Southwell can come from an analysis of sires.

The Table below shows the strike rate of sires at Southwell. The sample is restricted to those sires that had 30 runners or more. Again there is a huge contrast between the sires, with the off-spring of Mayson, Shamardal, Harbour Watch, and Society Rock having a terrific record on the fibresand. In comparison you have sires like Captain Rio, Arcano, Aussie Rules, Bertolini, and Excellent Art that have an absolutely shocking record at Southwell. Punters beware!

Table: Strike rate of sires in all-weather races at Southwell

Sire	Wins	Runs	Win %
Mayson	15	64	23.0%
Shamardal	10	51	20.0%
Harbour Watch	9	46	20.0%
Society Rock	6	30	20.0%
Kyllachy	15	78	19.0%
Pivotal	8	43	19.0%
Speightstown	7	37	19.0%
Poet's Voice	15	82	18.0%
Street Cry	8	44	18.0%
Lilbourne Lad	7	39	18.0%
Makfi	7	38	18.0%
Key Of Luck	6	34	18.0%
Big Bad Bob	6	33	18.0%
Bahamian Bounty	8	47	17.0%
Equiano	10	63	16.0%
Aqlaam	7	43	16.0%

Sire	Wins	Runs	Win %
Dandy Man	10	68	15.0%
Fastnet Rock	6	41	15.0%
Medicean	8	56	14.0%
Zoffany	5	37	14.0%
Exceed And Excel	7	55	13.0%
Royal Applause	7	55	13.0%
Piccolo	6	48	13.0%
Approve	6	47	13.0%
More Than Ready	4	32	13.0%
Invincible Spirit	9	77	12.0%
Monsieur Bond	14	114	12.0%
Holy Roman Emperor	5	41	12.0%
Assertive	4	33	12.0%
Kodiac	10	90	11.0%
Zebedee	6	54	11.0%
Showcasing	5	46	11.0%
Dark Angel	7	68	10.0%
Rip Van Winkle	5	51	10.0%

Sire	Wins	Runs	Win %
Dream Ahead	3	31	10.0%
Iffraaj	5	57	9.0%
Fast Company	3	34	9.0%
Bated Breath	3	32	9.0%
Acclamation	7	84	8.0%
Oasis Dream	4	69	6.0%
Captain Gerrard	4	62	6.0%
Camacho	3	53	6.0%
Milk It Mick	2	32	6.0%
Tamayuz	2	32	6.0%
Bushranger	2	31	6.0%
Helmet	2	31	6.0%
Sakhee's Secret	2	31	6.0%
Kheleyf	4	80	5.0%
Pastoral Pursuits	4	80	5.0%
Compton Place	2	40	5.0%
Captain Rio	1	40	3.0%
Arcano	1	33	3.0%

Sire	**Wins**	**Runs**	**Win %**
Aussie Rules	1	31	3.0%
Bertolini	1	31	3.0%
Excellent Art	1	30	3.0%

4 THE PUNTER AND THE BOOKMAKER

You still read a lot of nonsense about bookmakers being the old enemy of the punter and the uneasy relationship between them. The modern punter is both a backer and a layer and exploits the opportunities offered by the betting exchanges to back and lay each and every horse in a race.

This isn't to say that bookmakers are no longer relevant. I personally think that they are an important part of the game and atmosphere created by the betting ring at a racecourse definitely enriches the experience of a day at the races. Indeed It is more fun to place a bet with a bookie than it is to place a bet on your mobile. However, when you next place a bet at the racecourse you need to observe what goes on behind the back of the bookies satchel. More often that not you will find some sitting with a laptop computer and entering the bets into a piece of software that allows them to hedge your bet with other punters on the betting exchange.

In the twenty-first century the betting market is no longer the betting ring at a racecourse. It lives in the digital cloud, with people trading with each other on the outcome of races. Some may call themselves punters and others may call themselves bookmakers but the distinction has become blurred and people can interchange between roles in the blink of an eye. The modern backer needs to be able to exploit the opportunities that this new world creates.

Betting on the Exchanges

To give an example of how the betting exchanges have revolutionised the world of betting, I was at the races the other day with a few mates and we were cheering home a couple of 20 to 1 shots winners. This wasn't because we had backed them, but because we had layed a couple of short priced favourites to decent stakes on the exchanges in the morning. This is because the exchanges have allowed punters to become bookmakers, and turned bookmakers into punters. You can change your role from race to race or play both roles at the same time. There are simply so many more opportunities to make money from betting since the advent of the exchanges.

You do not simply have to back and lay to make money. There are plenty of people who trade prices on exchange markets to make profits regardless of which horse wins or loses a race. These traders are operating like stock market readers and are trading in and out of the market and making money on fluctuations in the odds. For example, if you see a horse plummeting in odds then you can make a trade by backing it at one price and then laying it a second later at a shorter price. You could make these trades scores of times on the same horse or you could trade other horses in the same race if their odds started moving in one direction or another.

The betting exchanges effectively encourage this form of activity because it brings increased liquidity, as large sums are constantly brought in and out of the market. This strategy has clearly been a success because Betfair matches 15 times as many daily transactions as the London Stock Exchange and like the London stock exchange these transactions are all digitised. One of the key reasons for the increase in transactions on the betting exchanges was the decision by BetDaq and Betfair to allow computer boffins to produce programs that can access something called the betting exchange API, which is jargon for basically allowing a computer a direct line into the exchange, making it possible to make scores of bets within seconds. It also allows one to play computerised betting strategies.

You don't need to be able to program a computer to make use of this innovation. The opened minded policy of the exchanges has resulted in some great software that allows less computer minded types to trade in a fairly sophisticated way. There are lots of products in this area. Bet Angel software is worth a mention because this company provide a free product called Bet Angel Basic that enhances the Betfair website interface. The software allows automatic refresh of odds and features a 'green-up' option that is a useful tool for guaranteeing that you make a profit out of race, regardless of the outcome, provided that you have a successful trading position.

Exchange trading though is just one possibility for making a profit. I know of some big punters that mainly play the in-running markets. They like to back big at very short odds on horses that look certain to win, provided that they don't do a Devon Loch or Dayjur inside the last few yards. As the latter examples testify this form of betting isn't for the faint hearted but if you have rapid reactions you can steal some money out of the market. But beware…

I'm certainly not going to tell you that it is easy to make money from betting on the exchanges. For the uninitiated there are plenty of ways to lose your shirt, and I for one have spent plenty of money on shirts in my time!

As I suggested earlier betting in-running is a specialised form of betting and to be honest I haven't really made it work for me. Certainly I've had success. I once got into the mindset that I had discovered the key to the mint when I started to play the in-running markets. I simply bet big on what looked like near certainties and must have landed scores of successful bets. However, you only need one or two mistakes if you are backing 1 to 20, 1 to 50 or even 1 to 100 shots!

When betting in running I think the most important thing to know is to know thy self. I know that I'm a greedy fellow and so I can come unstuck when I'm winning. For instance, when I started to make what looked like easy money I couldn't get enough of it. Thus, it simply wasn't good enough for me to back winners or to lay near certain losers' in-play. I had to back the winners and the placed horses in every race as well. This isn't a good plan because the level of concentration required simply isn't sustainable. It was only a matter of time before I made a mistake and after a few reverses I realised that this form of betting wasn't for me.

Trading has advantages over betting in running because you can get out of a position if it starts to turn on you. This cuts your losses. Therefore one of the most important tips when trading is to know when to get out and to take it on the chin. The most successful trader will be the one who knows when to get out and quickly recovers their composure to make their next trade. The trader who attempts to chase losses should read Nick Leesons Rogue Trader and conclude that this isn't a good idea!

Basically the betting exchanges have revolutionised betting in this country and have created many more opportunities to make your betting pay. For instance, it is well known that the Betfair SP offers better value than the industry SP. The modern backer basically needs to have an exchange account, and ideally an aptitude for computer programming or at least the knowledge to use the available software.

The psychological pitfalls of betting for a living

Betting on horse racing is tough. That is not to say that it is not enjoyable but it isn't easy and it requires great mental strength. However, most people who decide to bet seriously pay little attention to the psychological aspects of gambling and like to think that they are resilient enough to survive the inevitable losing spells and believe that they will not be affected by them or winning streaks. I can tell you, and I have seen this many times, that would-be professional backers that start off with that attitude rarely make it.

In my experience there are several psychological pitfalls that face punters, and if you want to make it as a successful backer you need to develop strategies for dealing with them. This requires one to think though the issues in advance and then have a plan of action for dealing with them as they arise. Like every good scout will tell you, be prepared!

One of the biggest psychological problems in punting is confidence. I don't mean confidence in terms of dealing with people or handling difficult social situations because one of the big advantages of betting for a living is that you don't need to deal with other people unless you want to! You don't need to worry about getting on well with your colleagues or sucking up to your boss. You are the boss and you can do all your interacting via a computer if you wish. Therefore, what I mean by confidence is having the belief that your methods are good and robust. You need to have this belief if you are to make it as a pro-backer because if you don't' you will give up too easily.

Naturally, we all differ in self-confidence and if you are weak in this area you need to compensate by basically doing more research, more testing and building up more evidence that your methods do work until you *really* believe in them. The pitfall here is that you might be so lacking in self belief that you only ever test your methods and never actually get around to implementing them. That is fine and I know plenty of people who never progress beyond the research phase of their betting project. At least they haven't lost any real money, and if they enjoy the research and analysis then the time isn't wasted either.

Having too much self belief can also obviously be a problem if you implement methods that you haven't worked through or you get carried away with them by over staking.

If you are one of these impulsive characters that have a huge ego then the bookies will love you! I recall going racing with a guy who really felt that he knew it all about the horses and was full of him self. In fairness he had enjoyed a good run and had come to the view that this was down to his brilliance. Before the first race he went up to a well known rails bookmaker and told him that he'd have his satchel bare by the end of the afternoon. Inevitably he left the track penniless and never picked up a racing paper again. If you are one of these characters, and if you have the insight to know that you are, then my advice is to paper trade for a while.

Paper trading is about making your selections in real time but you don't actually bet real cash. If you like to brag about your winning bets then tip them as well to your friends. This will give you a buzz if your methods are right but will give you the wake up call that you need if they prove not to work. There is nothing so ego deflating as having mates complaining about your terrible tips, and you will soon be cured of your over confidence.

Another vice is laziness. We are all lazy to some degree but if you are of the attitude that all you need to do in order to pick winners is to open up the *Racing Post* and scan the runners and riders then you are on the fast track to the poor house.

Maybe you're the sort of character who really can't be bothered with pain staking research but has all the other attributes to make it as a pro-backer. In that case, and as long you recognise this, then the easy solution is to get others to do the spade work for you and get expert advice. You should never be too proud to take advice. We can all glean new ideas or benefit from the skills of others. For example, I have good IT and statistical skills that I can apply in my betting research. Plenty of other people have these skills but there are many who do not, and if you fall into the latter category team up with someone who has those skills.

If you have developed sufficient confidence in your methods, and have purged yourself of any hubris, then you are ready to start betting for real. This brings on two further psychological pitfalls: winning and losing runs.

The winning run doesn't sound like much of a problem! However, it is the psychological impact that it can have that might lead you down the wrong path. Let me give you an example from my own experience.

I had developed a system at University that I had tested and it worked well. It didn't produce spectacular profits but it produced a consistent rate of return on past results and I had even paper traded the system for a time, and it had again shown a modest but reasonable level of profit. Satisfied that I had a good system I decided to implement it for real. It had a spectacular start that far exceeded anything like the returns that I had observed on the historic data. The first bet won, then the second, third and fourth. Okay I thought a good start but nothing more. Then bets five, six and seven all won as well. I was now starting to get excited and started to believe, despite all the past performance data I had on the system, that maybe the method was better than I had realised. Up to this point I had been betting to level stakes but when bets eight, nine and ten all won as well, and I was flush with the profits of 10 consecutive winners, I decided to abandon my staking plan and treble my wagers. Bet 11 went in and I felt so clever.

I won't bore you with what happened next because you will have realised that boom soon turned to bust, and after the next 6 bets went down I had wiped out not just all of my profits but, because I was now on treble stakes, I was now deep in the red.

Winning runs can therefore be dangerous if you let them influence your betting behaviour. If you have a carefully worked out strategy you need to stick to it.

The losing run has obvious perils. It can knock your confidence which can have all kinds of implications. Firstly, a losing run might lead you to abandon a fundamentally good strategy, especially if you had high expectations. It is better to start with a totally pessimistic attitude and be pleasantly surprised than to have an expectation of quick and easy profits. It is always a good idea to manage your expectations by setting aside a specific betting bank for your system and to assume that the money is already lost even before you have your first bet. Make sure the bank is big enough to sustain the maximum losing run you are prepared to absorb, and if the bank runs dry then that is the point at which to abandon the system.

In summary betting for a living involves much skill and judgement but in order to make a career out of it then you need to be your own psychologist as well. The skilful player who knows himself is the one who will come out on top.

Great betting coups

Serious betting is mainly a psychological battle. I know from bitter personal experience that a losing losing run can make you doubt your strategies and your ability to read the game. You can be left wondering whether your losing run is the result of bad luck or down to a bad system. A more nagging feeling is whether you are wasting your time. Can you really beat the layers? At times like these it is good to get inspiration from stories of those that have made it and those that have had that life changing win. I therefore want to provide you with a few uplifting tales of punters landing some colossal coups, and a couple of bold near misses.

Frankincense (1968 Lincoln Handicap)

Barry Hills announced his retirement in 2011 from the training ranks after a distinguished career in which he saddled countless Group winners and sired his own dynasty of top class jockeys. However, what is less well known is that his story began when he landed a monster gamble in the 1968 Lincoln Handicap.

The Lincoln is traditionally the curtain-raiser to the turf flat season and there have been some memorable gambles down the years but none were bigger than the coup landed on John Oxley's Frankincense in 1968. Barry Hills, who was Oxley's head lad, won so much money that he was able to set himself up as a trainer in his own right. In the years that have followed I'm sure Hills landed other hefty gambles, but he is not the only one to have had the bookies running for cover…

Forgive n Forget (1983 Coral Golden Hurdle Final)

Forgive n' Forget will be remembered by most punters as the runaway winner of the 1985 Cheltenham Gold Cup winner. However, to most bookmakers he will be most associated with winning the 1983 Coral Golden Hurdle Final, and for landing one of the biggest gambles in Festival history for his owner Tim Kilroe and trainer Jimmy Fitzgerald. The winnings that day were simply colossal and could probably have paid off the Greek national debt.

Despite a massive field, Forgive n' Forget was backed off the boards and jockey Mark Dwyer never looked concerned about the outcome on the 5-2 favourite, waiting until approaching the final flight to deliver his challenge and quickly mastering main market-rival Brunton Park to win by an easy three lengths. To this day the Kilroe coup is one of the biggest pay-outs at the Festival, and I'm sure many bookmakers in the ring wished they had never set off for Cheltenham that fateful day. They might have forgiven but they certainly won't forget!

Sadly the story didn't end happily for connections because, while Forgive n Forget gave them many more glorious days, he was fatally injured in the 1988 Cheltenham Gold Cup.

Destriero (1991 Supreme Novices Hurdle)

Irish owner Noel Furlong claims to have netted more than £1m when Destriero won the 1991 Supreme Novices' Hurdle at the Cheltenham festival. The horse was unexposed and came to Cheltenham with just the one run over hurdles under his belt – victory at Leopardstown on Boxing Day. His lack of form made certain that a nice big price was available on the the day of the big race. Trainer and owner could step confidently into the ring to get their money down as only they knew exactly how good the horse was.

Unfortunately, despite being fancied in many subsequent races, Destiero was somewhat disappointing after his festival success, although connections probably didn't care as he had more than paid for his carrots.

Pasternak (1997 Cesarewitch)

If your life depended on landing the odds in the 30 runner Cesarewitch Handicap at Newmarket then you would want Sir Mark Prescott on your side. The Baronet has always been the grand master of laying a horse out for a big handicap and boy did he land a coup for connections with

Pasternak in the 1997 renewal.

Pasternak was part-owned by the late Graham Rock, the first editor of the Racing Post and fearless punter. By some accounts he is said to have taken an amazing £5m out of the ring as the horse was backed off the boards from 11-1 to 4-1 on the day of the race. The outcome was never in doubt and the masterminds behind the coup were able to start counting their winnings well before George Duffield past the winning post.

Istabraq (1998 Champion Hurdle)

JP McManus has landed some pretty hefty bets at the Festival. His normal wager is a large detached house, and when he really gets stuck in it is either going to be a good or a bad day for the Irish balance of payments. Not all his coups have done to plan and when the Jim Dreaper trained giant Harcon finished second in the Sun Alliance Chase in 1995 his pockets were considerably lighter. However, McManus was undeterred and came back to land one of his biggest bets when Istabraq won the first of his three Champion Hurdles in 1998.

In what now looks like a remarkable display of generosity by the bookies, Istabraq was priced up at 14-1 to win the Champion Hurdle after winning the 1997 Supreme Novices Hurdle in impressive style. McManus and trainer Aidan O'Brien knew they had a great horse on their hands and they backed their judgement in hard cash and backed their horse at all prices down to 3-1.

The favourite duly kept his half of the bargain and coasted home from the opposition. It was an amazing day for McManus and for Irish racing fans, and the performance of the winner lives long in the memory.

Top Cees (1999 Chester Cup)

Jack and Lynda Ramsden took the bookies to the cleaners on numerous occasions but one of their boldest coups was with a horse called Top Cees in the 1999 Chester Cup. This was a controversial win because the horse had under performed on his previous run. This had some punters and racing hacks grumbling that they had been put away by trainer and jockey Kieran Fallon. They wouldn't have been complaining had they been 'on'!

Papillon (2000 Grand National)

The first winner of the Grand National was a horse called Lottery and looking through the races roll of honour there was never a more appropriate named winner of a horse race. In the years that have followed there have seen several shock winners of the National, at prices of up to 100-1. However, despite fields of 40 runners, 30 daunting fences, and a marathon race distance the Grand National has been the subject of several massive betting coups down the years and the bookies ended up on the receiving end of a right touch when Papillon landed the odds in the 2000 National for trainer Ted Walsh. On the morning of the race the horse was available at 33-1. The money poured onto him right up to the off, and he went off as the 10-1 joint second-favourite.

Monty's Pass (2003 Grand National)

Another National coup was landed when Mike Futter landed the mother and father of all gambles when his own horse Monty's Pass won 2003 renewal.

Futter, together with his four co-owners, is reported to have netted £1m plus, with individual bets of £5,000 each-way at 33-1 and £10,000 each-way at 20-1. Mr Futter had well and truly stuffed the bookies, which lifts the spirits because the major firms have been ripping ordinary punters off for years in the National, betting to huge margins on the starting price.

Denman (2007 Royal & Sun Alliance Chase and again in the 2008 Cheltenham Gold Cup)

Harry Findlay once lost £2.3 million on a single bet on New Zealand in the Rugby World Cup and so when he puts his money down he doesn't mess about. When his own horse Denman won the 2007 Royal & Sun Alliance Chase at the Cheltenham Festival he absolutely cleaned up and the winner was backed off the boards. However, this was nothing compared to the gamble landed in the 2008 Gold Cup when Denman put up one of the greatest ever performances to beat his legendary stable companion Kauto Star in what must be regarded as one of the finest races every seen at Prestbury Park.

Yellow Sam Bellewstown Handicap Hurdle (1975)

It would be a major omission not to include a betting coup from Barney Curley. Mr Curley started life as a priest, and to this day devotes himself to charitable causes. However, he has displayed little charity towards the bookies, whom he has fleeced on numerous occasions. He remains to this day a man the bookies genuinely fear. He pops up to collect a big pile of cash every couple of years, and reportedly landed a big touch on the all-weather last winter.

In 1975 Curley was already known to bookmakers and was finding it difficult to get money on. This presented a problem because Curley badly wanted to back a horse that he owned called Yellow Sam in a minor race at an obscure Irish course called Bellewstown.

The horse had been primed to win the handicap hurdle race at the little Irish track with military precision. His preparation had been to run in a series of races at other tracks in unfavourable conditions. This helped get the horse fit but, more importantly for Curley, disguised the horse's true ability from both the handicapper - which allowed Yellow Sam to race off a low handicap mark at Bellewstown - and from other punters.

In the days before mobile phones, Curley ordered his men to back the horse in bookies across the country in a series of small bets. This would help put the bookies off the scent. However, the bookmakers intelligence system was sure to realise eventually that they faced colossal liabilities from these small wagers if Yellow Sam won and would seek to back the horse at the track in order to reduce the price and to limit their office liabilities (sometimes termed "laying-off").

The problem for the bookies was that they needed to be able to contact their counterparts at the track in order to start laying-off. But Bellewstown racecourse was remote and crucially had only one telephone. This wasn't just bad luck. Curley had chosen the location of his coup for this very reason.

To prevent news filtering back to the course from bookmaker's offices, a friend blocked Bellewstown's sole phone box with an apparently urgent call. This prevented off-course bookmakers from getting messages through to their representatives at the track with instructions to start backing the horse. Yellow Sam duly obliged at 20-1, landing Curley more than £300,000, the equivalent of more than £1.7m in today's money.

The coup made Barney Curley famous throughout Ireland and the United Kingdom, and made headlines in many Irish and British national newspapers and television reports.

Curley, like Barry Hills after his successful coup on Frankincense in the 1968 Cambridgeshire, invested his earnings in a training establishment in Newmarket from which he primed his own horses for specific gambles. He also purchased Middleton House, a mansion in Mullingar, County Westmeath, which he later sold off in a raffle that netted £1million.

The Yellow Sam coup by Curley reveals him to be a true punting genius and while some may grumble about his tactics no laws were broken. He was just too clever for the bookies.

The attempted coup on Gay Future

In landing the Yellow Sam coup Curley must surely have learned a few lessons from the attempted coup on Gay Future one sweltering hot August Bank Holiday in 1974.

Anthony Collins, a trainer based in Scotland, entered Gay Future for a race at Cartmel at their August meeting. The date and location were not accidental. Cartmel is a small racecourse in a remote location in northern England, and the August Bank Holiday fixture list is traditionally one of the busiest days in the racing calendar to the extent that most national newspapers don't have space to print the runners and riders for minor meetings such as Cartmel.

While Gay Future was declared to race at Carmel, Collins had also entered two other horses, Opera Cloak and Ankerwyke, in races at other courses later in the day. He then conspired with his accomplices to place a vast number of small bets, backing Gay Future in a doubles and trebles with either of the other two horses. Bookmakers wouldn't normally associate these kinds of bets with a coup and so a £10 or £20 win double wouldn't attract much attention, especially on a busy bank holiday Monday. However, under bookmakers own rules, if you place a win double on two horses, and one of the horses is a non-runner the bet automatically becomes a win single. Collins therefore pulled out both Opera Cloak and Ankerwyke from their respective races and so all the doubles and trebles now became a colossal win single on Gay Future.

Gay Future's form was dreadful and he looked fully exposed. Few punters would have wanted to back him but nevertheless soapy flakes were rubbed into the legs of the Gay Future to give the impression the horse was sweating and to keep on-track punters from backing it, holding its odds of 10-1.

The horse duly romped home but following an investigation, Collins and an Irish building contractor Tony Murphy were convicted of conspiracy to defraud the bookmakers and fined. They never saw any of their winnings.

The investigation revealed that Murphy and Collins had won the race at Cartmel with Gay Future, but the horse who had been racing under the name Gay Future in all his previous races in England was another useless nag. Meanwhile the real Gay Future was being primed for the Cartmel race by ace trainer Edward O'Grady. The two horses were then switched on the way to Cartmel.

Collins and Murphy would have won millions, and they almost got away with the coup. Unfortunately the trainer Collins didn't follow the agreed plan. He was told by Murphy to take Opera Cloak and Ankerwyke to the races but to break-down on the way. However, he left both horses at his yard, and so when his secretary answered an apparently innocent inquiry from a journalist about the well being of Opera Cloak and Ankerwyke it was obvious that they had never actually left their stables in Scotland and that Collins had always intended for them to be non-runners.

In some ways Collins and Murphy were a bit too clever for their own good, and went too far in order to land the coup. In a complex plot they had breached the rules of racing and broken the law. The case went to court and the bookmakers wanted the maximum sentence for the duo. It was clear that both were guilty but curiously the judge was sympathetic and let them off with a slap on the wrist. I doubt he was in on the coup but he probably didn't like the bookies moaning about being had. This fascinating story was made into a television film in the late 1970s.

I hope these tales of great betting coups have lifted your spirits. If they inspire you to set up your own coup then I wish you the very best of luck in 2020.

Can you really win millions by using a betting system?

Can you make your betting pay? This is the question that occupies most punters minds. The reality is that for the majority of backers the answer is a big, bank busting ‘no’. However, there are plenty of players that make a decent profit out of the game. I don’t have any hard evidence but my view is that the number of winning punters has been growing in recent years, especially since the advent of the betting exchanges, and there is now a decent sized pool of professional gamblers.

Certainly the betting exchanges have made a big difference as the over-round or margin of profit made by layers on each horse has had to be reduced in order to attract backers. The other big development has been the reduction in the price of a computer. Over recent years the cost of a PC has plummeted and one can now buy for a few hundred pounds a processor capable of grinding though millions of calculation per second, or handling huge amounts of data. A new generation of punters has embraced the new information technology. There is now a strong market for specialist software that can place bets for you according to the strategies that you want to select, and you can also buy software that allows you to study of form and conduct data analysis on thousands of horse race performances. The modern punter is therefore more informed and more sophisticated than his predecessors.

The most advanced players are now regularly using electronic form databases to develop systems and then using or developing programs to place bets on the system selections, and using models to calculate the size of bet to place on each horse. I have been fascinated by these approaches for many years and I developed my first computer based betting system when I was in secondary school and barely out of short trousers. My subsequent efforts though, while successful, look prehistoric when compared to the efforts of the Hong Kong betting syndicates.

Computer based betting and wagering systems have reached the pinnacle of sophistication in Hong Kong and there are a number of high-tech teams competing with each other for profits. However, the story of computer-assisted betting in Hong Kong begins with Bill Benter. He is said to take home around $37 million a year via his computer based betting operation.

After graduating from University, the highly numerate Benter quickly realised that it was much more fun making money from gambling than from an average job. His first gambling venture though concerned cards and not horses after he discovered *Beat the Dealer* in the mid-1970s. For those not familiar with this book it is basically a bible for blackjack card counters. He memorized the best-selling book's strategies and hit the casinos in Las Vegas. This wasn’t popular with the casinos and after a seven year winning streak he was banned.

Benter's ban from the casinos might have been the end of his gambling story had he not encountered a fellow card counter called Alan Woods. Woods interested Benter because he not only shared the same unusual occupation but had an in-depth expertise in horse racing that complemented his own mathematical modeling and computer programming. Conversations between these two great men led them to conclude that it was possible to make money from applying mathematical models to horse racing. They became racing partners and in 1984, moved to Hong Kong to implement their methods.

Equipped with a $150,000 bankroll provided mostly by Woods, the two card counters planned to apply the theories of winning at blackjack to winning at the races. Success wasn't instant and it is interesting to read that the beginning was difficult. The original model used by Woods and Benter only considered 16 variables for each horse and they were using pencil and paper to collect the data. By the third season they had computerised their system, allowing historical results data to be analysed. However, they didn't make a profit for five years. This is revealing because it shows that you need to persevere to make a profit from horse racing. Most successful business people will tell you that instant success is rare and that it can take many years to make a profit from a product. It would seem that computer based betting follows a similar path.

The rewards though, when they did eventually come, were well worth the wait. Once the model was accurately identifying the probabilities of each horse in every race the returns were massive. The partnership between Woods and Benter broke up shortly after the system became profitable after disputes about money management. This though didn't really do either of them any financial harm as both would became highly successful computer based handicappers in their own right. Woods sadly died in 2008 at the age of 62 and his fortune at the time of his death was estimated at $670 million.

One interesting question about the Benter/Woods project is why did they both focus on horse racing in Hong Kong when both were US citizens? The number of horse races in the US is also vastly more than in Hong Kong which would presumably have given them more opportunities to boost their turnover. It also seems a pretty radical decision to leave your homeland and set up a betting operation in a country far from home which you know very little about. It is speculation but the pull to Hong Kong must have been driven by some underlying factors about horse racing in Hong Kong that suggested to them both that the chance of making a profit was greater than in the US or any other racing jurisdiction.

My guess is that Benter and Woods specialised in horse racing in Hong Kong because it has a closed horse population i.e. the same 1,000 or so horses compete against each other throughout the season, which helps keep things consistent. The number of tracks, unlike in the US or the UK, is very small and all courses follow a similar layout and have a similar surface. Perhaps more significantly the betting pools (and Hong Kong only has pool betting) are also massive and dwarf those in the US or the UK. This means that if a syndicate can cream off just 1% of the total betting pool then they will be making vast sums of money. There might also be something to be said about the quality of bets placed in the Hong Kong pools as the vast majority of betting on horse racing is by recreational players who may not even study the racing form. This would give the more sophisticated player – and you don't get much more sophisticated than Woods and Benter – a big advantage.

How does the Woods/Benter system work? Woods has probably taken his secret of success to the grave, and Benter and his associates are unlikely to spill the beans. However, we know that Woods and Benter both constructed a computer model designed to estimate the winning probabilities of each horse in every race. In Benter's later models, this involved the investigation of 120 different handicapping factors and the writing of some 750,000 lines of computer code. The model then tells the team the appropriate amount to bet on each horse and the bets are then submitted into the betting pools.

In order to develop the model Benter employed state-of-the-art statistical forecasting techniques. He has written about some of these in a classic paper entitled *'Computer based horse race handicapping and wagering systems: a report* published as a chapter in *The Efficiency of Racetrack Betting Markets*. That paper reveals that his method has been to identify each individual factor that could possibly predict the outcome of a horse race. He has then worked to whittle these factors down to the most reliable and effective. Once he had a model that worked on past data, he tested it 'out-of-sample; i.e. on a large sample of further races. Interestingly he sometimes found that a variable was useful in predicting race outcomes but he really couldn't understand why that should be the case i.e. it didn't conform to any known racing logic. In such circumstances, he decided the best policy was not to care. Faced with a choice between a profitable model that he couldn't fully explain, and an unprofitable model that he understood perfectly, he chose the former. This pragmatic approach clearly works, although purists will struggle with this. Over the years he has refined his model and has hired academics specialising in statistics from Ireland, Las Vegas and Boston to serve as consultants presumably to improve its performance.

The bedrock of the betting system, and the factor behind any successful computerized betting operation, is access to vast quantities of accurate data. If you don't have data you can't hope to develop a successful model and the success of Bill Benter resides in a massive collection of data on each horse - including details about the tracks and jockeys. Data doesn't come cheap and the data bank needs constant updating. Benter, for example, has employees whose sole job it is to review race tapes after every meeting. They judge each horse on 120 characteristics - attributes like speed during the first third of the race, whether it got bumped coming out of a turn, the quality of its recovery from the bump, and, of course, how it finished. This information goes into the database, where it can be cross-referenced and called up to help predict the outcome of any impending race that a particular horse runs in. It is interesting that Benter chooses to collect his own data in this way, which must be very expensive, rather than rely on published sources. For instance, in the UK most of the information that Benter is collecting could come from the official form book or the *Racing Post*. Benter must be gaining a competitive advantage in obtaining information that only he has access to. Provided that his data is of better quality than published sources or is unique then he gains an advantage over other players. This advantage must be big enough to justify the effort and expense.

Given the fantastic success of Benter and Woods a number of other betting syndicates have set up in Hong Kong and competition between them is fierce. Technological secrets are closely guarded, nobody's keen to publicise their betting strategies, and the cagiest players aim to hide their wagers from other teams - all of which monitor the flow of racing money via an independent online service called Telequote, based in Hong Kong. This increased level of competition must have lowered profits and I doubt whether Benter is making as much as he did before the advent of other computer based syndicates. This isn't to say that he isn't still making substantial profits. I've read enough about this remarkable guy to believe that he will always find a way to stay ahead of the crowd.

Overall, I find the story of Alan Woods and Bill Benter absolutely fascinating. Both men are clearly gambling legends and an inspiration to anyone that wants to bet profitably on horse racing. Obviously we can't all be geniuses like these two men, or have access to the resources to set up a betting operation as sophisticated as that of Woods and Benter, but if anyone tells you that you can't make a profit from betting on the horses then please tell them this tale.

Punters need better data

I have little interest in football but I was surprised to learn recently that all of the premiership club in England employs a statistician or a team of statisticians to analyse the performance of every player at the club and across the league. The clubs have made a significant investment in data analysis and buy-in huge amounts of information from a range of sources.

The data reveals a vast amount of information about players and their performance, such as how many goals a player has scored, how many completed passes, the number of successful tackles, number of goals saved, number of interceptions, number of fouls committed, etc, etc. No matter what factor you can come up with these clubs probably have data on it. However, it is no good having huge amounts of data unless you can analyse it.

The statisticians are employed by the clubs to provide briefing to managers, coaches and the club executive on which players are performing well, and which areas of their game they need to improve. The benefits here are obvious if you think about how this could help improve the efficiency of the clubs training. However, the research could also be used to help in team selection by helping to deploy those players that would be best at implementing a certain tactic. For example, if you are the manager and you want to play a long ball game against an opposing team that you think is weak in the air, then you can use those players from your squad that the data tells you are the most successful at winning headers, and controlling the ball from the air.

The statisticians are not just analysing data on their own players. They are also using information to reveal weaknesses in their opponents, and this analysis can be used to shape team tactics. The statisticians are employed to develop and implement techniques to quantify the ability of players on a range of football skills, and to use these metrics to compare one player against another. This reminds me of a computer game I played as a kid called ‘Football Manager’. This gave every player a rating in different domains, such as whether they were good at attacking, making passes, defending or saving goals. I recall my excitement when I had the chance to ‘buy’ the top rated striker Ian Rush, and to pair him with Gary Linker upfront. What a combination! That computer game – and all those other football management games that have come out since – have now become reality and actual premiership football teams are using hard statistical data, and player ratings to not only pick their teams, but also to put a monetary value on players.

Premiership football is now big business. Teams need to win matches to keep themselves in the premier league, and this is crucial if the club is to retain the enormous revenues that come from being a premiership club. The Clubs therefore need to invest in the best players, but they don’t want to pay over the odds. The statisticians are helping to come up with metrics to enable clubs to quantify the respective merits of players and economists are using this research to put a financial value on their heads. This helps the club to identify new players that may be undervalued in the transfer market and who might represent a good investment, or to smoke out players that are overvalued and to negotiate their price down to a level that better represents their true value.

As I said before I'm not very interested in football and those of you who are more enthusiastic about the game may have known this already, but I've become surprised about how sophisticated football clubs have become. I'm perhaps stuck in the past and recall managers who were either long ball merchants or, as Brian Clough would say "played football on grass". Today's coaches would appear to be playing the game not by instinct but by numbers. In some ways premiership football in this country has come to realise the potential of data, and worked out how to use it effectively, far later than in the United States. In American Baseball the data revolution came some time ago, as anyone who has seen the film *Moneyball* will testify. However, when it comes to data, horse racing in the UK isn't even off first base.

The data revolution in football has no doubt been a great boost for quantitative minded football punters, who can use the same data available to the football clubs to help predict the result of football matches. Whether or not this has been the catalyst for the massive growth we have seen in football betting in recent years in an open question but I'm sure it must have helped to some extent as it brings a new type of punter into the game. The rise of football betting has also been a threat to the horse racing industry, which derives much of its funding from betting. This is because more and more of the betting pound has had to be shared with football. Therefore horse racing needs to be enticing punters away from football betting and get them backing on horse races. The availability and quality of data and statistics could be important here as punters want to make informed choices before making a bet. If football offers better information to punters than horse racing then it becomes a more attractive sport to bet on.

Horse racing has a longer history of trying to quantify the ability of racehorses. For example, since the advent of the Timeform organisation in 1948 punters and form experts have been trying to quantify the ability of races horses using race times. Indeed the history of quantification in horse racing probably goes back to Admiral Rous, who in the 19th century came up with the first set of handicap ratings. The official handicap ratings compiled by the British Horse racing Authority are the latest version of these ability ratings. However, while horse racing was centuries ahead of football in using data to create ability ratings, it has been very slow to collect, record new types of data and to make this information available to racing professionals and punters.

As a racing fan it is sad to say that football looks to have embraced the data revolution and now provides huge amounts of information on players. In contrast the horse racing authorities keep punters in the dark when they could turn the lights on and put so much more data into the public domain. For example, punters in the UK do not have access to sectional times for all horse races. This is a hugely important form factor that has become routine information to US punters who use this information to work out the likely pace of a race, and which horses are likely to gain uncontested leads. In my book *'Pace Wins the Race'* I managed to work out a way to provide similar information to UK punters using the limited information that is available in this country, but US punters get this information routinely.

In fairness to the BHA they have attempted to quantify the ground conditions at tracks more scientifically, but I don't think racing experts have any confidence that the official going reports are any more reliable or that they are recorded in a consistent way across racecourses. This is a major problem because the going is such an important form factor. This is basic information that needs to be properly recorded.

In Hong Kong and in other countries punters also know the weight of the horse. This data is collected by weighing each horse prior to racing and this information is made available to punters so that they can judge whether the horse has grown or is in race fit condition, such as whether it is significantly under or over weight. Again this crucial information is not available to punters in the UK. It would only take a modest investment to collect this information and it might also help to improve the integrity of the game (i.e. it might help to stamp out the practice of running an unfit horse in a race to bring down its handicap mark!)

It is about time the racing authorities in this country woke up to the data revolution that is occurring in other sports and started to realise that the modern punter wants more and better information before he or she places a bet on a sporting event. Punters basically want to see new and innovative statistics on racehorses and their performance, otherwise people will prefer to bet on football, and this will eventually cost the sport billions.

However, while I definitely think that horse racing needs to provide punters with better data, I'm not sure this is necessarily in the best interests of the winning punter, at least in the short-run The fact that most punters in the UK are flying blind when it comes to studying the form gives an advantage to those that take the time to get most out of the data that is available, or come up with their own unique statistics. For example, those that take the trouble to study horse and trainer patterns, and develop an original set of statistics, can sometimes gain an edge over their fellow punters. If you have the resources then you can also gain an edge by buying in subscription data that isn’t widely available and can be used to give you an edge, or pay for original research that might give you a new way to use existing data. Winning punters though make their profits from the losses made by other punters, and if the supply of losing punters is reduced because people want to bet more on data rich sports like football then, in the long-run, that is no good for everyone.

5 THE TIPSTER

The racing tipster has been one of the few constants over the decades, and tipsters have been around since racing began. Most are useless but some aren't and one of things that has changed this century is that there is now more information available to be able to differentiate between those tipsters who genuinely know something about the game and those that don't.

The Racing Post have for many years produced statistics on the main newspaper tipsters and report on the percentage of winners that they select and the level of profit and loss that they record across the year, broken down between their naps and regular selections. Across all selections none of the newspaper tipsters in my experience has ever shown a profit across the year, although some have shown profits on their naps but there is seldom any consistency. A tipster might record a profit in one year but will seldom follow-up with profits the following year. The newspaper tipsters are always unlikely to make a profit at SP odds because so many people follow their selections and whatever edge (if any) that they have quickly gets incorporated into the odds.

There are though some exceptions and one of the modern

phenomena has been the advent of the Pricewise tipping service in the Racing Post. This column has a fantastic following and any horse tipped up by Pricewise can be expected to shorten dramatically in the betting.

Pricewise

In terms of background the column is currently headed by Tom Segal. He took over from Mel Collier as Pricewise in the summer of 2001. Before that Segal had written news pieces and had been Spotform on the Racing Post as well as standing in as Pricewise when Collier was on holiday.

In the summer of 2005, Tom Segal had an exceptional winning streak, with winners tipped on 10 consecutive Saturdays. The Racing Post and the national press reported how Pricewise was so influential that his tipping even dented the profits of high street bookmaker, William Hill. The then Chief Executive of William Hill, David Harding, even told shareholders that profits would have been a lot better "if it wasn't for Pricewise". On the back of the success of the Pricewise column in the Racing Post newspaper the Racing Post website launched Pricewise Extra in February 2009. This was a paid subscription service to members of the Racing Post website that paid a premium to receive the service.

What does the data tell us? In my survey of Pricewise selections over a four year period I found that the Pricewise column in the Racing Post newspaper had a strike rate of around 14 per cent, which isn't terribly good when you consider that if you backed every favourite in every race you could expect to have more than one winner for every four bets placed. However, Pricewise isn't concerned with strike rate because a good strike rate doesn't necessarily translate into profits. For example, if you backed every favourite you would back plenty of winners and record a high strike rate, but you would lose about 10 to 15 per cent of your stakes.

In one of the years surveyed Tom Segal made a profit. His rate of return at the Betfair SP was around 35 per cent. This is a great rate of return at SP. The following year though his rate of return slumped to 21 per cent. Not bad but the level of profit is clearly been eroded. Sure enough by the following year of the survey all the profit from Pricewise selections had gone. It looked like a case of Tom Segal being a victim of his own success and that his selections have basically become over bet so that the value has gone out of his tips. He would no doubt argue that he identifies value bets from the tissue prices offered by the major bookmakers. This is fair comment and his performance would have been better to his advised odds, but whether one can actually get on a decent bets at his advised odds is doubtful. The Betfair SP is therefore a reasonable guide as to the profitability of his selections, although the early birds among you with an accommodating bookmaker may be able to beat the market.

The risk though one takes is that Pricewise is capable of producing some shocking losing runs. Within the my survey period he had one sequence of 38 consecutive losing selections! The Racing Post didn't put that on their front page! Indeed long losing runs are common place when betting on Pricewise because he has a low winners to runners strike rate.

Overall it appears that these days backing Pricewise selections to win at the Betfair SP is likely to return a modest profit at best, and it is a risky strategy given Segal's low winning strike rate and tendency to have long losing runs. However, is there another way to profit from Pricewise?

In the twenty-first century the betting exchanges make it possible for punters to be both backers and layers. A popular strategy among the more sophisticated punter is to trade his selections. The method is simple enough: bet the Pricewise selection at the best odds available (i.e. as close to his advised price as possible), then wait till it shortens a little further and lay off on the exchanges. This strategy is based on the tendency for his selections to shorten in the betting. The first price drop tends to happen after around 8.30am on a Saturday. The price then often drifts downwards as the late-morning punters get on at whatever prices they can. Some selections will continue to shorten throughout the day till the off. The potential therefore definitely exists to bet first, then lay off later at shorter odds for a small profit. The returns are small but frequent. One needs to be smart about it because I've noticed that at the very big festival meetings the odds on Pricewise selections hold up because the markets are so strong for other fancied runners. This seems to be especially true at the Cheltenham festival which has hyper strong markets, formed by knowledgeable and more serious punters. This is important to note because a good proportion of his selections are made at the big festival meetings.

The other obvious limitation of a trading strategy on Pricewise selections is that the more people who know about it and use it then the less likely it will be to work in the long-run. The other limitation is that to make any decent money one needs to try to get an information edge over other punters (that is a general rule to successful punting) and because the Pricewise selections are public information then the only edge one can obtain is to access selections before anyone else, or at least the majority of his followers. This is obviously hard unless one is either a) Tom Segal or b) works for the Racing Post and gets sight of the selections before they are made available. Neither of these options is available to me and you and so the best alternative is to get up very early to get the selections online (which requires a subscription to the Racing Post tipping website. Not cheap) or get a copy of the Racing Post newspaper hot off the press. If you like to sleep in on a Saturday morning then this strategy probably isn't for you!

Newspaper naps

Racing correspondents in the press have had a hard time of it in the twenty-first century. The rise of the internet and falling newspaper sales has cut the number of column inches in newspapers devoted to horse racing and reduced print advertising has meant that a number of racing correspondents has fallen markedly over the last twenty years. Their workload though hasn't declined because there is now so much more racing for them to cover, and while the life of a racing correspondent is enviable compared to the jobs most of us have, it certainly isn't easy to work your way through the form book, assess a race and put up a selection in every contest. Indeed I did recently see an interview with a racing hack who said that the time he gets to study a race and put up a selection is literally a few minutes in order to meet print deadlines.

The naps of newspaper tipster though are different. I'm told that newspaper editors keep note of racing correspondents naps and like to see their correspondent near the top of the Racing Post naps table. It gives the newspaper bragging rights if it can advertise good priced winning naps and a fair amount of pressure is put on tipsters to turn in decent priced winners even if they don't show an overall profit on all their naps. This produces a healthy competition between the tipsters, and they consider their naps more carefully than their run of the mill selections, and only give nap status to the horse they genuinely think is the horse most likely to win from all the selections they have put up that day.

The statistics provide some evidence for this. Horses napped by at least one newspaper tipster win much more frequently than horses that are not. Napped horses win at a rate of about 24 per cent whereas horses that don't receive the honour of a nap win at a rate of just just 10 per cent. In other words horses that get a nap are nearly two-and-a-half times more likely to win than a horse that hasn't been napped. The downer on this statistics is that the strike rate isn't high enough to compensate for the the lower odds on newspaper naps. A bet on every nap in my database would result in a loss of over five per cent on capital invested at the Betfair SP (less 5% commission on all winnings).

The picture becomes more rosy when we consider horses that received five naps or more. This means that at least five newspaper correspondents from either the national, large local newspapers or the racing press have to put up the same horse as their nap. and so if a number of tipsters select the same horse it must have a better chance of winning than others in the race. The strike rate of these horses is an impressive 43 per cent, although the odds recorded for winning selections is around 11/8 whereas for horses with one or more naps the odds for the winning selections is roughly double this figure. In terms though of profit and loss my data shows that you would break exactly even on these selections after paying the give per cent commission on all winning. Not a profit but in comparison to a lot of systems and tipsters this isn't a bad record.

Another approach favoured by some punters I know is to bet on the horse that have received only one solitary nap. The logic here is that the tipster might know something that the others tipsters don't because they have a connection with the stable or some other unique piece of information. The statistics though show that this is a recipe for the poor house and you would record a six per cent loss on turnover betting on these selections. The solitary nap is therefore to be avoided.

The analysis so far suggests that newspaper tipsters aren’t exactly money spinners. The modern punter though can also be a layer and you might be able to trade a profit by backing a newspaper tipsters nap in the morning and then laying it at a shorter price at the off. The logic here is obvious enough. A horse that gets a newspaper nap is going to be on most punters watchlist and it might influence some to back that horse. The more punters that follow the tipster the more likely it will be for the odds to fall. The first step to assess this hypothesis is to see of newspaper naps make a profit or a smaller loss if you back them at the morning line odds, and test whether the average morning line odds are higher than the SP price taken just before the start of the race.

In my analysis I take the morning line price on Betfair to be the average weighted trading price at 11am on the morning of the race, with at least £100 traded. This basically is the average back price taken on all bets made on a horse prior to 11am. As a result of the restriction about only calculating the average price on horses that have at least £100 bet on them prior to 11am, some horses do not have a morning line price and for analysis purposes these selections are ignored. This doesn’t exclude many horses from the sample but it does knock out a few cases at minor mid week meetings, especially evening races that don;t take place for some hours after 11am.

Now that these details are out of the way what does the analysis show us? Not a lot. The average morning line price on nap selections is about the same as the final SP odds. This basically means that the morning line prices fully reflect all the nap information. Horses that have a nap therefore don;t shorted in the betting. This means that a trading strategy on them won't work. The same result occurs when you only consider those selections five naps or more.

Is there any profit to be had from newspaper naps? There definitely isn't any profit in betting naps in handicap races. These are as difficult for newspaper tipsters as they are for the rest of us and the average newspaper tipster records a nasty seven per cent loss on naps in handicap races. In non-handicap races the loss is reduced to around three per cent after commission. When you restrict selections to only those horses with five or more naps in non-handicaps you do slightly better than break even after commission.

I did consider only looking at the Racing Post tipsters. The rationale here is that the Racing Post tipsters must be better informed than most other tipsters because they are living and breathing racing everyday and working with colleagues that only focus on horse racing and tipping. Surely they must be picking up information that is useful for picking winners? The statistics suggest otherwise. The trade press basically do a bit better than other tipsters but the odds are shorter in their selections. This means that an edge can't be found and therefore you can't make a profit from their advice in the long-run.

The limitation of newspaper tipsters is that they have to put up selections the day before a race and therefore they cannot take account of changing situational factors like changes in the going or changes in riding arrangements and other factors that might change from when they send off their copy to their editor and when the race starts. They are always behind the information curve and don't even have the betting market to guide them for most of the races that they study (the exception being big races with strong ante-post markets). The advantage that they might have in terms of superior skill in form analysis is lost because once their tips are published everyone has access to that information and therefore the information gets baked into the odds on offer. The only way one can therefore benefit from using a tipster is using a service that doesn't make its selections public. These private tipsters might give you an edge because not everyone will have access to the information that they offer.

Do Racing Post Top Speed selections represent value bets?

I've always had mixed feelings about speed figures. On the one hand they make intuitive appeal in that surely the horse that has previously demonstrated that it is the fastest must be the most likely winner? The facts though suggest otherwise and collateral form ratings like the Racing Post Rating get a higher proportion of winners than the same newspapers speed rating expert named Top Speed. Indeed some years ago the Racing Post withdrew Top Speed ratings from the all newspaper tipster competition because the selection of Top Speed always seemed to make a big loss.

In comparison speed figures are the backbone of serious form analysis in the United States. Andy Beyer, author of the best selling Picking Winners, was one of the early proponents of speed figures and came up with a method for comparing horses performances on the clock over different distance and track conditions. That methodology is pretty much the standard way of comping speed figures and the so called Beyer Speed Figures have a very high strike rate in the US, and horses with the best speed figures generally go off as favourites because speed figures are so good at marking out which horses have the best chance in a race.

The question though is why do speed figures work so well in the US but less so in the UK? There are probably two main reasons. Firstly, races in the US tend to be run at a fast pace throughout and that produces more reliable times. In contrast races in the UK, especially on the turf, tend to be more tactical affairs. Secondly, track conditions in the US are more uniform in that the tracks are pretty much identical and that makes it easier to compare times over different courses. This is not the case in the UK, where every track has its own particular characteristics.

The underfoot conditions are also more uniform in the US because almost all races take place on dirt or synthetic surfaces. This is a big difference to turf racing in the UK when the going can have a big impact on finishing times, and can vary from very slow heavy ground to super quick firm going. These differences probably make it much harder for speed handicappers in the UK, especially given other problems such as unreliable race distance measurements and race times.

The problems facing speed handicappers in the UK though are reduced when it comes to assessing the speed of horses on the all-weather tracks. The number of courses is limited and it is generally the same population of horses competing against one another at each track, especially in handicaps. The underfoot conditions are also less variable as there are only three track surfaces operating in the UK, namely Polytrack, Tapeta and Fibresand. Times are also more reliable in flat races in comparison to jump races and all-weather racing is entirely flat based (the experiment in the early 1990s with jump racing on the all-weather was quickly abandoned due to equine fatalities). Therefore if speed figures are to work in the UK then they are most likely to work on the all-weather.

Is this true? What do the statistics tell us? In flat handicap races in 2019 the horse with the highest master Racing Post Rating won at a rate of 15 percent in turf races but only 13 per cent on the all-weather. In contrast, the horse with the highest Top Speed rating won 13 per cent of the time in turf races but had a strike rate of 15 per cent in all-weather races. In other words speed ratings did better in all-weather races and did better than collateral form ratings on this surface compared to turf races. Speed figures therefore look the way to go on the all-weather.

Speed figures on the all-weather appear to be less reliable when the surface is described as slow. In handicap races the horse with the highest Top Speed rating won at a rate of 16 per cent when the going was described as 'standard' but that strike rate dropped to 14 per cent when the going was recorded as 'slow or standard to slow'.

The track surface can also vary by whether it is Polytrack, Fibresand or Tapeta. Polytrack and Tapeta are supposed to be similar and equivalent to good to firm going on the turf. Lingfield, Chelmsford, and Kempton use Polytrack whereas Wolverhampton and Newcastle race over Tapeta. Southwell on the other hand uses Fibresand, and is basically a deeper surface that is regarded a similar to soft going on the turf. Top Speed seems to do best at Southwell and Wolverhampton recording strike rates of 20 and 18 per cent respectively. At Kempton and Chelmsford the strike rate for Top Speed selections is around 15 per cent. However, for Newcastle (10 per cent) and Lingfield (12 per cent) the strike rate is much lower. The lower strike rate for these course can't be explained by differences in field sizes as all the courses in the all-weather family have roughly the same average number of runners.

In terms of race distance there didn't seem to be much of a pattern in term f strike rate, even when I looked at distances by each course. It is therefore difficult to explain why Top Speed does relatively poorly at Newcastle and Lingfield. It is easier to explain why Top Speed does better at Southwell. These is a Fibresand track and the slowness of the surface would suggest that speed figures would be less reliable under these conditions. However, the deepness of the surface makes it hard for horses to accelerate past each other and so races tend to be run at a true end-to-end pace and this might make the times of horses a more reliable measure of their ability because race tactics are probably less important.

In terms of profitability is you backed the Top Speed selection in every all-weather handicap at the Betfair Starting Price (ignoring commission) you would record a loss of 5 per cent on turnover. However, you would do slightly better if you backed only the horse with the highest RPR. That would make you a loss of just 4 per cent. This implies that punters have already recognised that speed figures are better on the all-weather and you aren't getting an edge.

There is though a way to reduce losses. When you restrict your bets to only those horses with a Top Speed figure higher than the horses handicap mark your loses reduce to just 2 per cent but when you do the same for the RPR selections losses are still around 4 per cent. This suggests that speed figures are useful in identifying well-handicapped horses, and this information isn't entirely baked into the odds to the same extent as other publicly available information, such as RPR ratings.

Timeform star ratings: what are they worth?

Timeform is probably the most well-known form analysis service in British horse racing. It was founded by Phil Bull in 1948 to provide profitable information to punters and others involved in the horse racing industry.

The unique selling point of Timeform in it's early days was that Phil Bull wanted to establish a mathematical relationship to a horse's performance, based on the time the horse recorded. This made Bull and Timeform a pioneer in the use of speed ratings. Later Bull started publishing a racing series, which evolved into the Racehorses and Chasers and Hurdlers annuals. In 2006 the company was purchased by the sports betting exchange Betfair in December 2006 for a reported £15 million.

Since being taken over by Timeform the organisation has provided an excellent free-to-view website, and expanded on its product range. The company has also syndicated its services to a range of media. This means that AtTheRaces and the Sporting Life websites now carry something called Timeform form summaries and Timeform Star Ratings. These free form summaries and ratings are now also carried by a number of newspapers. However, as far as I know no one has undertaken an analysis of their performance. In this Chapter I have analysed the performance of the Timeform ratings since they became available in 2004 for British and Irish racing.

Firstly I should point out that the free Timeform Star ratings are not the same as the Timeform form ratings. The latter are only available as a subscription service and are basically handicap ratings, similar to the Racing Post Ratings and Top Speed services provided by the Racing Post. The free Timeform star ratings though should have a decent winners to runners record given that Timeform employs some of the best form analysts in the country and is the University for racing professionals. For instance current Channel Four racing pundits Jim McGrath and Graham Cunningham are past alumni of the Halifax based organisation, with McGrath being a one-time managing director of the company.

Given the expertise available at Timeform then one would expect them to produce plenty of winners. The fact that they have to produce a star rating for every horse in every race run in Great Britain and Ireland, day in and day out, probably means that they are very unlikely to make an overall profit at Starting Price odds. The acid test for them is about whether they out perform the record of the Starting Price favourite.

What are the Timeform Star ratings? The ratings are very simple. Every horse in a race is given a rating between 0 and 5, and this includes half points as well. In other words Timeform place each horse in a race on the equivalent of a 11 point scale (0, 0.5, 1, 1.5, 2, 2.5, 3, 3.5, 4, 4.5, 5) . The horse with a five star rating is the one they think will win the race.

In my analysis I've focussed on jump races run in Great Britain and Ireland from 2004, and recorded the odds and finishing position of all horses that had a star rating. I've focussed on jump races simply because the jump race season is about to get into full swing. At some point in the future I might consider the results of flat races.

How do the ratings perform? My statistics show that from 40,850 runners that had a five star rating 9,150 managed to win. That represents a strike rate of 22 per cent. This is clearly much better than random because if you simply closed your eyes and stuck a pin into a race card you could expect to record a strike rate of around 9 per cent in this same sample of races. The ratings are also good at discriminating between runners because horses rated zero performed less well than the average runner, recording a strike rate of just 7.9 per cent. In contrast the horses rated with 4.5 stars had a winners to runners ratio of around 16 per cent, with all the other points on the scale recording a strike rate between 7.9 per cent (0 stars) and 22 per cent (5 stars), with a linear relationship between stars and the percentage strike rate. In comparison, the Starting Price favourite records a strike rate of something around one winner in every three selections (33 per cent). This is considerably higher than the Timeform top-rated.

The number of winners to runners and the percentage strike rate are not the be all and end all. The critical test is whether or not Timeform ratings do better than the Starting Price favourite in terms of profit and loss. Simply backing the Starting Price favourite in every race would net you a loss of around 5 per cent on turnover. Not great but not that bad, and I know a lot of punters that lose a lot more than that! Alas, the Timeform ratings would appear to do worse than the SP favourite in that simply backing the five star rated selection would net you a loss of 16 per cent on turnover.

Okay the story on Timeform Star Ratings isn't looking great so far, but maybe they do better on some types of races than others. I considered the statistics on all chases, handicaps and non-handicaps. Unfortunately the results were the same as the average reported above. The exception was hurdle races. The loss on these types of races (handicaps and non-handicaps alike) was just nine per cent. I can't think of any good reason as to why Timeform might do better with hurdle races than any other type of race and so I'm included to think that this is just a statistical fluke rather than anything more important.

In summary, Timeform Star Ratings are free to use and readily available from a variety of websites and newspapers. They do identify more than their fair share of winners in that they do much better than picking a horse at random from the race card. Unfortunately they don't perform as well as simply blindly backing the starting price favourite.

6 THE RACECOURSE

The twenty-first century has seen a number of changes to the number and nature of British racecourses. At present we have 59 racecourses operating in Great Britain. This doesn't include Folkestone, which was mothballed several years ago until a decision is made over its future. It currently looks a sad feature in the Kent countryside.

We did lose Hereford racecourse in 2010 but fortunately it reopened in 2016, but Towcester racecourse is currently in administration and the future of racing at the venue looks uncertain. Kempton racecourse currently has the sword of Damocles hanging over it. In 2017 the Jockey Club announced the closure of the course by 2021 to make room for a housing development. This would see the King George VI Chase and Christmas Hurdle moved to Sandown Park racecourse, with the other jumps fixtures to be spread around other Jockey Club-owned racecourses throughout the country while the all-weather track would be replaced by a new artificial track to be built at Newmarket.

These developments are not new. Racecourses have struggled to compete for the leisure pound, especially in more remote rural locations. The almost endless rise in house prices has also made the land on which they are situated more and more valuable. These economic pressures look likely to continue. It remains to be seen whether this will lead to more racecourse closures in the twenty-first century but in the twenty-first century racing lost scores of racecourses to the developers.

All-weather racecourses

It is not all gloom and doom. Some may disagree but one of the more positive developments for me in the late twentieth century was the advent of all-weather racing across a number of tracks. This looks like a growth area in the twenty-first century.

In the 1980s the UK experienced a number of really cold winters that put paid to large chunks of the turf programme. This led to the first all-weather tracks opening at Lingfield and Southwell in the early 1990s. Originally flat and jump races were run on the all-weather but a succession of equine fatalities in jump races resulted in flat-only racing.

All-weather tracks have proved to be a sound investment. In the twenty-first century the all-weather now makes up a significant part of the overall racing fixture list. The quality of the races and the horses has improved significantly and you now see group level horses running on the all-weather, and the races now attract runners from the top stables.

Synthetic track surfaces, unlike turf, are hard wearing which means that more meetings and more races can take place, and this results in more revenue for racecourses and for the racing industry. The proven success of

Southwell and Lingfield led to the opening of more tracks at Wolverhampton, Kempton, Chelmsford and Dundalk in Ireland. It remains possible that more tracks might open n the years ahead. It should also be noted that some jump courses are putting in stretches of all-weather surface on areas prone to waterlogging. For example Fontwell has put in a large all-weather strip on one of its bends and that course as a result can host more fixtures throughout the winter.

All-weather tracks though are not all the same. For instance, Southwell races on Fibresand whereas the other tracks race on the more modern Polytrack and Tapeta surfaces. This makes a difference to the way in which races are run and attract different types of horses, with different going preferences. Southwell rides very much like good to soft or softer types of going on turf whereas Lingfield, Kempton, Chelmsford and Wolverhampton are regarded as favouring horses that favour good or faster types of ground. The kickback at Southwell is also much greater than on the Polytrack and Tapeta courses and this can unnerve some horses when they race there for the first time. The tracks also differ in their configuration and this can produce varying degrees of draw bias.

While all-weather races are now of much better quality than in the past, the day-to-day mid-week racing is still very much low grade stuff. I prefer to bet on handicap races on the all-weather as these tend to attract better quality animals than claimers and sellers, although the lowest quality handicaps will often comprise horses that have been running in selling class races. The higher class handicaps will sometimes attract horses capable of running in stakes races because there are still few high class stakes races for the best all-weather performers and so they are often forced to run in handicaps. Classier horses tend to run to form more often and so handicaps tend to be more predictable than lower class races and that is why I have concentrated on these races.

There are some general form factors that help to narrow down the field in all-weather handicaps. The betting market is one of the best guides because inside information is particularly important at this level. Thus if a horse shortens markedly in the betting it is often because the stable and owners have lumped on. This is more prevalent in all-weather racing because the betting market is often weak and so big bets have more of an influence on the reported odds, but also because of the economics of all-weather racing. The economics are such that if an owner or trainer doesn't bet then it is difficult to see how they can make the game pay. The owners playing the all-weather game are some leagues below the likes of Coolmore and the Maktoums and the prizes on offer are more the equivalent of a clapped out second hand car than a top of the range four-by-four. As far as I can work out successful betting is the only way to balance the books. Astute punters who follow the market movers can therefore latch onto this inside information.

However, it is often difficult to know how the market will move in advance of a race. A good guide here is the starting price recorded by the horse on its last race. The statistics show clearly that the shorter the odds last time out the more likely a horse is to win next time. The reasons for this are not clear but it might reflect the fact that if a horse was fancied last time then it must have had something in its favour. Connections may have also got their fingers burnt and may prime the horse to recoup their losses at the next available opportunity. Therefore my advice is to keep your eyes on the betting market and the price the horse started at last time out.

At the lower echelons of the racing world there is often not a great deal of difference between any of the competitors. Consequently small advantages can make a big difference to the outcome of a race. Recent fitness is a key example. A horse that has run recently is more likely to win than a horse that is returning to the track after a break or returning from injury. You should downgrade a horse's chance according to the number of days it has been off the track. This information is available from any national newspaper and it is one of the most important factors.

The official handicapper seeks to weight horses according to their ability. The most able horses carry the most weight. This can put them at a disadvantage and so you should make some adjustment to the chance of a horse according to the amount of weight it being asked to concede to its rivals. However, you need to be cautious here because the official handicapper allocates the most weight to the most able horses and so you must also take this into account in your final assessment (my systems seek to do this for you – see below).

The handicapper may also apply special penalties to horses that have won well last time out but are retuning to the track within seven days before he/she had had the opportunity to re-evaluate their handicap rating. Statistically a handicap penalty is a positive signal. It indicates that the horse may be ahead of the handicapper i.e. shown a level of recent form that exceeds its current rating. The statistics show that the extra weight is insufficient to reduce the horse's likelihood of success. Racehorse trainers are also not stupid and they will exploit this advantage. For example, if a trainer enters a horse in a race with a seven-pound penalty he probably thinks that the horse has at least that in hand and this negates the extra burden. He or she will then run the horse as many times as they can before the animal is re-assessed and required to race in higher class races or off a higher handicap rating. In short, the higher the handicap penalty the better the horses chance.

Southwell

As mentioned earlier Southwell has a Fibresand surface. This produces a large amount of kick back and the transition from turf or Polytrack to Fibresand can often unsettle a horse. The statistics show that you need to downgrade the chance of a horse running on Fibresand for the first time. It will be at a disadvantage compared to rivals that have had previous experience of the surface.

Good recent form is also a positive. The best way to assess good recent form is by the Racing Post's handicap rating (the RPR). The horse that recorded the highest RPR on its last outing has the best chance. However, you should also consider the RPRs for each of the horse's last three performances and note the highest figure recorded. This 'best of three' figure should be compared to that recorded by all the horses in the race and the horse with the highest 'best' figure should be respected.

The recent form of the horse is obviously important but punters often overlook the form of the trainer. It seems rather obvious but a trainer that hasn't had a winner from his last hundred runners is either useless or the stable is suffering from some sort of virus that has caused its horses to under perform. You want to avoid runners from these stables and concentrate on those that have had a recent winner. The Racing Post contains information on the number of runners a trainer has had since a winner and this is often a good guide as to whether or not the stable is in or out of form.

The draw is often an important factor on the all-weather tracks. In the early days it used to exert a huge influence. For example, at Lingfield a low draw was fatal because the then Equitrack surface used to roll down a slight gradient towards the inside rail. This used to make the going deeper for those horses with a low draw and seriously hinder their chance. These major biases have largely been eradicated either because of structural changes to the track or (as was the case at Lingfield) the type of all-weather surface was changed. Nevertheless biases do still exist on some tracks because of the track layout. All-weather courses are often smaller than turf tracks in order to reduce the cost of the artificial surface and also because the all-weather track has had to be laid inside an existing turf track. This means that the course can have a number of tight bends, even over short distances. Unlike in athletics horse races do not have staggered starts and so horses drawn closest to the rail have the least distance to travel. This means that they can gain an edge of a few lengths over their rivals, and this can often be decisive.

However, while I have conducted much research into draw biases at the all-weather tracks I cannot find a clear bias at Southwell. Certainly some draw positions have recorded more winners than other positions but once you control for the number of runners in the race and the characteristics of the horses then there doesn’t appear to be any significant bias.

A system can be developed from the form factors we have discussed for races run at Southwell on the all-weather. I have attached weights or scores to each of these factors to reflect their influence. The horse with the highest total rating is the most likely winner or the horse most likely to be placed.

1. Take the decimal odds recorded by the horse on its last race (the SP) and multiply this by (minus) -1 points. This is to reflect the fact that the higher the SP last time out the less chance the horse has of winning or being placed today.

2. For every day since the horse's last race multiply the number of days by -0.3 points. The horse that has been off the track for the most time will record the biggest negative value to reflect the fact that it is probably unfit.

3. If the horse is carrying a penalty multiply the penalty by +9 points.

4. If the horse is makings its debut on the Southwell Fibresand you should deduct 18 points from its score. It probably won't like the kick-back.

5. Rank each horse according to the Racing Post Rating (RPR) that it earned for its last race and multiply the rank (1 being the rank of the highest rated horse) by -12 points. The horse with the lowest RPR will record the biggest negative value because it performed the worst of all the runners last time out.

6. Rank each horse according to the best Racing Post Rating (RPR) that it earned from its last three race and multiply the rank (1 being rank of the highest rated horse) by - 16 points.

7. Rank each horse according to its current official BHA handicap rating (1 being rank of the highest rated horse) and multiply by +6 points. Thus, the lower down the weights the more points the horse should receive.

8. Find out the number of runners a trainer has had since he/she last

had a winner. Take the number of runners since a winner and multiply this figure by – 0.4. This factor should capture the trainers recent form and ability.

When combined these form factors produce a final score for each horse which is a good indicator of its chance. The horse with the highest rating is the most likely winner or most likely to be placed. The system returns a decent strike rate and while it may not pick the winner of every race it does help to narrow down a field to a few live contenders.

Kempton

There is a definite draw bias at Kempton and horses drawn high have a significant bias. Thus the higher the draw the greater the horses chance of success. This is my system for Kempton. Note the weightings on the variables differ from Southwell. This is a system designed for Kempton only.

1. Take the decimal odds recorded by the horse on its last race (the SP) and multiply this by (minus) -1.4 points. This is to reflect the fact that the higher the SP last time out the less chance the horse has of winning or being placed today.

2. For every day since the horse's last race multiply the number of days by -0.2 points. The horse that has been off the track for the most time will record the biggest negative value to reflect the fact that it is probably unfit.

3. If the horse is carrying a penalty multiply the penalty by +4 points.

4. Rank each horse according to the Racing Post Rating (RPR) that it earned for its last race and multiply the rank (1 being the rank of the highest rated horse) by -10 points. The horse with the lowest RPR will record the biggest negative value because it performed the worst of all the runners last time out.

5. Rank each horse according to the best Racing Post Rating (RPR) that it earned from its last three race and multiply the rank (1 being rank of the highest rated horse) by - 10 points.

6. Rank each horse according to its current official BHA handicap rating (1 being rank of the highest rated horse) and multiply by +4 points. Thus, the lower down the weights the more points the horse should receive.

7. Find out the number of runners a trainer has had since he/she last had a winner. Take the number of runners since a winner and multiply this figure by – 0.6. This factor should capture the trainers recent form and ability.

8. Multiply the horses draw position by +5 points

Wolverhampton

There is a definite draw bias at Wolverhampton and horses drawn low have a significant bias. Thus the higher the draw the greater the horses chance of success.

Here is my system for Wolverhampton.

1. Take the decimal odds recorded by the horse on its last race (the SP) and multiply this by (minus) -1.2 points. This is to reflect the fact that the higher the SP last time out the less chance the horse has of winning or being placed today.

2. For every day since the horse's last race multiply the number of days by -0.3 points. The horse that has been off the track for the most time will record the biggest negative value to reflect the fact that it is probably unfit.

3. If the horse is carrying a penalty multiply the penalty by +7 points.

4. Rank each horse according to the Racing Post Rating (RPR) that it earned for its last race and multiply the rank (1 being the rank of the highest rated horse) by -12 points. The horse with the lowest RPR will record the biggest negative value because it performed the worst of all the runners last time out.

5. Rank each horse according to the best Racing Post Rating (RPR) that it earned from its last three race and multiply the rank (1 being rank of the highest rated horse) by - 11 points.

6. Rank each horse according to its current official BHA handicap rating (1 being rank of the highest rated horse) and multiply by +4 points. Thus, the lower down the weights the more points the horse should receive.

7. Find out the number of runners a trainer has had since he/she last had a winner. Take the number of runners since a winner and multiply this figure by – 0.7. This factor should capture the trainers

recent form and ability.

8. Multiply the horses draw position by -4 points

Lingfield

However, while Lingfield's equitrack surface used to have a strong draw bias, the new Polytrack surface reveals no definite draw bias as far as I can tell.

As with the other courses I've developed a system for Lingfield.

1. Take the decimal odds recorded by the horse on its last race (the SP) and multiply this by (minus) -1.4 points. This is to reflect the fact that the higher the SP last time out the less chance the horse has of winning or being placed today.

2. For every day since the horse's last race multiply the number of days by -0.2 points. The horse that has been off the track for the most time will record the biggest negative value to reflect the fact that it is probably unfit.

3. If the horse is carrying a penalty multiply the penalty by +3 points.

4. Rank each horse according to the Racing Post Rating (RPR) that it earned for its last race and multiply the rank (1 being the rank of the highest rated horse) by -13 points. The horse with the lowest RPR will record the biggest negative value because it performed the worst of all the runners last time out.

5. Rank each horse according to the best Racing Post Rating (RPR) that it earned from its last three race and multiply the rank (1 being rank of the highest rated horse) by - 8 points.

6. Rank each horse according to its current official BHA handicap rating (1 being rank of the highest rated horse) and multiply by +1 points. Thus, the lower down the weights the more points the horse should receive.

7. Find out the number of runners a trainer has had since he/she last had a winner. Take the number of runners since a winner and multiply this figure by – 0.7. This factor should capture the trainers recent form and ability.

Goodwood

I was once at a Goodwood racecourse open day and some brave soul on the tour of the track surveyed the magnificent Sussex downs and asked the clerk of the course whether he had considered putting in an all-weather track. I thought the clerk was going to have a stroke! There certainly won't be all-weather racing at Goodwood. However, despite Goodwood being my local track and I've had many days there when I have wished they put in an all-weather course or knocked the place down for housing!

I find Goodwood a hard place to make money, and I know I'm not the only one. I think the reason why Goodwood can sometimes baffle punters is that it is comprises a number of different courses and each one has its own unique features. For instance, the straight six furlong course has an incline from the start, to the extent that it is impossible to see the runners at the start when looking down the track at ground level. It is then downhill towards the winning post. The 5 furlong course is one of the quickest in the country. Courses over longer distances take a number of bends, and are uphill to start but then have a downhill finish. The undulations and sharp downhill finish mean that the course is a bit on the sharp side and tends to suit speedy types.

The undulations on the track are also uneven and vary depending on the draw position. The six furlong course is straight, and therefore shouldn't really have a draw bias, but this track seems to favour certain stalls. This though is hard to work out without good statistics. .

Draw bias is an important factor and is one that the serious punter simply cannot ignore. However, it is very easy to misinterpret the effect of draw. One of the commonest mistakes is to make conclusions based on insufficient data. I have often watched the racing on television and heard the commentator make a statement about the draw from the result of just one race. This is easily done. I recall in particular a discussion about the draw at Newmarket during the Guineas meeting a few years ago. Horses drawn low had won one or two races and this led some to believe that there was a bias. But historical data based on many races, shows that Newmarket doesn't have a draw bias. The course is perfectly straight, with good drainage across the track. There is no physical reason why Newmarket should show a bias and the data backs this up. The fact that one or two races went to horses drawn low was of no real consequence. The results arose by chance.

In order to interpret the effect of the draw correctly you need large samples. These samples can be drawn at two levels: the race level and the individual level. I'll explain what I mean by this, starting with race level analysis.

Most people study the draw by looking at race level data. In other words they only look at the draw of the winning horse. Under this method all you need to do is calculate the proportion of the winners drawn in the top, middle and lower parts of the course. Therefore on a fair track each third of the track would be expected to produce a third of all the winners. This is because the draw positions are allocated at random, and one can therefore expect that, over a sufficiently large sample of races, the average quality of the runners is equal for each part of the track. For instance, you would expect that there would be as many good horses drawn in the high stalls as in the low stalls.

Evaluating draw bias based on the draw position of the winners appeals because it is easy to interpret. The problem is that it wastes a lot of data because it only focuses on the winners. If you get a few freakish winners (i.e. horses that won against the true bias) then you can completely misinterpret the data. This can be costly.

The obvious way of improving this method is to include more races by going further and further back in time. This builds up a bigger sample, and so you are less likely to be misled by chance results. The problem here though is that draw biases change over time. They come and go at particular courses due to the effect of changes to the layout of the track or to the drainage system. Clerks of the course are always trying to eliminate draw biases and such changes are common. Recent data is therefore preferable to old data, but a balance has to be struck between having recent data and having a sufficient sample size so as not be conned by freak results. If you go too far back you also run into another problem. From spring 2011 the racing authorities in their wisdom decided that punters needed to be confused further and they decided to change policy on stall numbers. This meant that stall numbering on right handed courses was switched, so that the inside stall is always stall number 1. This can make a nonsense of draw analysis using data from before 2011.

I therefore prefer to make use of recent data and increase the sample size by considering the performance of each individual horse in a race. This is what I mean by analysing the draw at the individual level. In other words you don't just consider the post position of the winner, but the lengths beaten by all the runners in the race. This method obviously increases the sample size because in a 10-runner race you can consider the position of all the runners and determine whether the draw influenced the number of lengths by which each horse was beaten. If you have data on only five races with an average of 10 runners this still gives you 50 observations to work from, rather than just 5. This reduces the probability of making erroneous conclusions from small samples.

Using this method I'm able to quantify the bias over the 6-furlong course at Goodwood . In the chart below you can see that horses drawn low are beaten less than horses drawn high. For instance a horse drawn 1 on average is beaten around 4 lengths but horses drawn high in stalls 25,26,27 are beaten by around 8 lengths. This is a 4 length difference and over six furlongs that is a massive amount of ground to make up. In other words if you ignore the draw you are at a disadvantage. You basically need a horse drawn high to be well-in at the weights to make up that kind of difference.

This analysis shows the power of my draw methodology because I'm not sure that you would spot this bias had you simply considered the draw positions of the winners over a few races. A few random results would completely throw you off the scent.

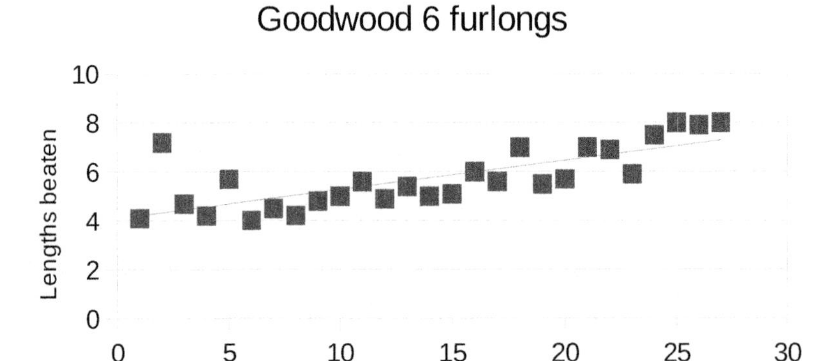

The hugely successful professional punter Patrick Veitch reportedly made heaps of cash by betting on draw biases. However, he is now of the view that the value has gone out of this method because draw biases are now so well known. I would probably agree that you can no longer make a long term profit by simply backing horses with certain draw positions at certain tracks. For example, bookmakers factor into their odds the draw position of horses running at Chester. However, I think that you need to still understand these biases and a few subtle ones still exist.

I wouldn't go as far to say that you should back the bias blindly. You need to combine knowledge of draw biases with other form factors. A significant one would be to identify horses with a good draw that also show early pace. These horses will be able to capitalise on a good draw. After all it is no good backing a horse with a fantastic draw if it has a reputation for being a poor starter. A pace setter at Goodwood over 6 furlongs with a good draw can be a useful combination, especially if they also have previous form at the track.

Pace wins the race…especially at certain tracks

Chester is a good example of a course that has a strong pace bias. York also favours horses that race up with the pace, especially when the ground is on the soft side of good. My records also show that over five furlongs Epsom, Windsor and Thirsk strongly favour pacesetters. In contrast pacesetters find it very difficult to win over five furlongs at Newmarket and Southwell.

It is difficult to isolate any one particular factor that would explain why one track is more favourable to pacesetters than another. Track configuration probably plays a part. For instance, York has a long sweeping bend into a straight on its eleven and twelve furlong tracks and this would seem to offer pacesetters some sort of advantage. The draw bias at certain courses is also probably an advantage to horses that set the pace because they are able to break from the stalls quickly and obtain a favourable position. This might explain why pacesetter enjoy such a good record at Chester, where it is important to get to the inside rail in order to take advantage of the tight bends. At some courses the underfoot conditions also tend to favour pacesetters. For instance, firm ground favours pacesetters and at Brighton firm ground often prevails because most of the course fixtures take place during the hot summer months (July and August).

Certainly front runners win more often at some tracks than others and this bias can be very strong. However, in order to profit from this form of track bias you need to be able to predict in advance which horses are likely to set the early pace. As described early in this book I have been compiling my own pace ratings for a number of years in order to work out which horse is most likely to set the early pace.

The Table below provides a summary of the courses that were profitable for horses predicted on my ratings to race up in a recent flat season. However, be wary of the small numbers! For instance the six-furlong track at Chepstow records a large profit but the sample includes only 9 runners.

Summary of the courses that were profitable for horses predicted to race up with the pace.

Dist (f)	Course	Lost	Won	Total runners	% Win	Profit/ loss (£)	Profit/ loss (%)
8	Ascot	41	6	47	12.8	0.5	1.06
10	Ascot	8	2	10	20	7	70
12	Ascot	15	2	17	11.8	6.5	38.24
6	Bath	159	18	177	10.2	7	3.95
8	Bath	79	11	90	12.2	96.33	107.04
7	Brighton	46	10	56	17.9	29.25	52.23
8	Brighton	21	6	27	22.2	10.11	37.46
6	Carlisle	8	1	9	11.1	2	22.22
7	Carlisle	7	2	9	22.2	2.75	30.56
12	Carlisle	4	2	6	33.3	8	133.33
6	Chepstow	7	2	9	22.2	35.75	397.22
8	Chester	8	2	10	20	1.1	11

Dist (f)	Course	Lost	Won	Total runners	% Win	Profit/ loss (£)	Profit/ loss (%)
12	Chester	8	1	9	11.1	6	66.67
5	Epsom	18	3	21	14.3	3.5	16.67
7	Goodwood	40	5	45	11.1	91.5	203.33
11	Goodwood	15	2	17	11.8	7	41.18
8	Haydock	2	1	3	33.3	3.5	116.67
5	Kempton	26	4	30	13.3	3.17	10.56
9	Kempton	16	2	18	11.1	11.75	65.28
12	Kempton	24	4	28	14.3	15.25	54.46
12+	Kempton	21	1	22	4.5	12	54.55
5	Musselburgh	76	12	88	13.6	4.88	5.54
7	Newcastle	63	5	68	7.4	107.41	157.95
8	Newcastle	19	4	23	17.4	2.75	11.96
12	Newmarket (Rowley)	15	7	22	31.8	33.25	151.14
6	Nottingham	63	9	72	12.5	6.22	8.65
6	Pontefract	55	9	64	14.1	0.07	0.11
12+	Pontefract	27	2	29	6.9	3.5	12.07
8	Redcar	30	1	31	3.2	3	9.68
9	Redcar	14	1	15	6.7	19	126.67
6	Ripon	61	13	74	17.6	45.77	61.85
12+	Ripon	35	6	41	14.6	12	29.27

Dist (f)	Course	Lost	Won	Total runners	% Win	Profit/ loss (£)	Profit/ loss (%)
5	Salisbury	22	4	26	15.4	12.38	47.6
6	Salisbury	21	5	26	19.2	3.94	15.17
5	Thirsk	54	8	62	12.9	3.7	5.97
12+	Thirsk	19	2	21	9.5	12	57.14
6	Windsor	57	11	68	16.2	1.13	1.65
11	Yarmouth	32	4	36	11.1	0.5	1.39
12+	Yarmouth	13	2	15	13.3	24	160
11	York	41	7	48	14.6	28.13	58.59
12+	York	7	3	10	30	17	170
Total		1455	221	1676	13.2	704.76	42.05

Watching horses in the racecourse paddock

One of the great advantages of going racing at a British racecourse is that you can get close to the, horses and there is plenty of information to be gained by watching horses in the parade ring or watching them canter to the start, provided that you know what signs you are looking for.

One major piece of evidence often overlooked by punters is the physical appearance of a horse in the paddock prior to racing. I have started to pay more attention to this information and have started to conduct some in-depth analysis into the subject, particularly on two-year-old debutants. In this Chapter I want to share with you some of my initial findings.

In the pre-internet age and in the era before dedicated racing channels, paddock observation could only be done at the racetrack. However, this information is now readily available to the stay-at-home-punter. For instance, Raceform Interactive includes paddock notes on horses making their racing debuts and/or where their specialist team of racecourse experts thinks there is something of particular relevance, such as a horse looking exceptionally well or out of sorts. The Racing Post is now providing live text updates on its website which often reports noteworthy information from the paddock. There is also the terrestrial and dedicated satellite racing channels that often give comment on the pre-race look of a horse. The trick here is to know which commentators actually know what they are talking about. You will have to form your own view on this. I don't want to get sued for libel!

Given all the information and expert comment one therefore doesn't have to know a great detail about the look of a horse to benefit from this source of information. However, one does need to know what pieces of information are important and which are not. A major clue here comes from some academic research that I cam across a few years ago.

One key study looked at the pre-race behaviour of horses as a predictor of race finishing order. The authors considered the look of around 900 horses and recorded a mass of data on their pre-race behaviour and appearance. Fourteen variables were recorded in the parade ring while the rest were scored while the horse was cantering to the starting gate. The results showed that winners tended to look fitter and were more relaxed and losers tended to be more aroused and required greater control by groom and jockey. Arousal could be detected by the elevation of the head, neck and tail. Thus a horse with a high head and neck carriage on the way to the start might be wasting valuable energy or might have a physical problem.

Interestingly the study showed that sweating didn't seem very important which runs against the conventional wisdom of many racing pundits that sweating is a sign of anxiety. The researchers found that it wasn't significant on its own but was moderately significant when combined with other negative factors like signs of arousal in the parade ring or on the way to the start.

However, the authors key finding was that pre race behaviour was an important part of the overall form picture, but it was only a part. The results showed that on its own the information was only moderately useful at picking winners (i.e. of only some value to backers). However pre race appearance was extremely useful in identifying losers, which makes the information of particular interest for those wanting to lay horses on the exchanges.

My own research has been on the paddock notes compiled by Raceform because the data is readily available from Raceform Interactive. However, an assumption can be made that a good paddock judge will arrive at similar conclusions to the Raceform experts.

One of my key findings is that two-year-old debutants that are noted as 'good sorts' deserve plenty of respect. From my analysis of 229 horses that recorded this comment in Raceform 32 went onto win. This represents a strike rate of 14 per cent, which is just about twice the success rate recorded by juveniles that didn't record this type of comment. However, juveniles improve for a run and so if you back horses noted as good sorts on their second run then, based on my sample, 191 'good sorts' raced for a second time in their juvenile year and 54 of them won ! This

increases the strike rate to more than 28 per cent, around twice the level recorded by ‘good sorts’ on their debut. You could also back ‘good sorts’ on their third run and you would record a similar strike rate.

Horses that are noted as ‘scopey’ are also worth careful consideration. This comment is usually reserved for horses that are of particular note and look to have potential. They are not quite the finished article but the basics are all in place and the horse may develop into something above average. Horses noted as having ‘scope’ on their debut win at a rate of about 10 per cent on their first run but, as you would expect of such horses, they improve markedly for the experience and on their second run their strike rate doubles to 20 per cent.

However, what about the negatives? A common comment recorded in the Raceform Paddock notes is ‘leggy’ or ‘leggy sort’. This basically means that the horse hasn’t grown into its frame and it is usually a sign of immaturity and the horse will need time to develop if it is to show its best. My data shows that of more than 1,100 horses that recorded this comment only 64 managed to make it to the winners enclosure, which is a success rate of less than six per cent and lower than the average strike rate of all runners. The comment ‘leggy’ can be interpreted as the same as the comment ‘unfurnished’, which also indicates an immature horse. Horses that recorded this comment recorded the same strike rate as ‘leggy’ types, which confirms that either comment is a serious negative. However, you need to be wary of laying these runners as they develop because as they grow through the season they will improve. Thus on their first run they record a hopeless strike rate; on their second run they do slightly better but from their third run onwards their strike rate is back up to the average.

You don't need to be expert or spend every day at the racecourse to be able to benefit from paddock inspections: simply make use of published reports. You can then spend your time processing the information and identifying the most useful pieces of information. The data could then be incorporated into winner finding systems or lay strategies.

Do some racecourses favour favourites more than others?

A few years ago I decided to do some research into the record of Starting Price favourites at certain tracks. I focussed my research on non-handicaps hurdles because in handicap races over the sticks you would have lost over 10 per cent backing the favourite but in non-handicaps you would have lost only around 5 per cent. However, even when I restricted my analysis to non-handicap hurdles over the last decade I found that the record of the favourite varied enormously between different tracks.

In Table 1 I have analysed the record of the favourite in non-handicap hurdle races by racecourse. As you can see there are no less than 25 tracks where the jolly favourite returns a profit.

Favourites at Cork do best in terms of rate of return, making a profit of nearly 17 per cent on turnover. The strike rate is also nearly one winner in every two selections. In contrast you wouldn't want to be backing the favourite at courses such as Thurles, Kilbeggan, Sligo, Fairyhouse, Aintree, Ascot or Killarney where the favourite has a strike rate of less than 35 per cent and losses of more than 20 per cent would have been made.

The hurdle track at Cork, Listowel, Ballinrobe, Sandown, Wexford,

Hereford, Haydock, Lingfield, Downpatrick, Huntingdon, Aintree, Windsor, Newbury, Taunton, Clonmel, Gowran Park, Worcester, Cheltenham, Navan, Musselburgh, Perth, Stratford, Kelso, Southwell and Doncaster are the ones at which one should be backing the favourite.

Had you backed every favourite in non-handicap hurdles at these courses you would have made 4,096 bets and would have backed 1,862 winners (45 per cent). This would have resulted in a profit of around £219 or a rate of return of just over 5 per cent on all stakes invested. This isn't a fortune by any means but it is a significant turnaround on the 5 per cent loss recorded by the favourite at all courses.

Table 1: The record of the favourite in non-handicap hurdle races by racecourse, (Great Britain and Ireland)

Course	Wins	Runners	%Win	Profit/loss(£)	Profit/ loss(%)
CORK	53	107	49.5	16.62	15.53
LISTOWEL	22	51	43.1	6.40	12.55
BALLINROBE	15	31	48.4	2.88	9.29
SANDOWN	73	157	46.5	14.26	9.08
WEXFORD	29	72	40.3	6.09	8.46
HEREFORD	167	362	46.1	29.72	8.21
HAYDOCK	100	222	45.0	18.17	8.19
LINGFIELD	41	86	47.7	6.80	7.91
DOWNPATRICK	28	70	40.0	5.03	7.19

Course	Wins	Runners	%Win	Profit/loss(£)	Profit/ loss(%)
HUNTINGDON	133	291	45.7	20.53	7.05
AINTREE	10	25	40.0	1.61	6.44
WINhDSOR	33	77	42.9	4.86	6.31
NEWBURY	102	240	42.5	15.13	6.30
TAUNTON	145	303	47.9	17.90	5.91
CLONMEL	36	89	40.4	4.47	5.02
GOWRAN PARK	33	77	42.9	3.31	4.30
WORCESTER	166	371	44.7	13.82	3.72
CHELTENHAM	26	53	49.1	1.93	3.64
NAVAN	47	102	46.1	3.05	2.99
MUSSELBURGH	70	144	48.6	4.26	2.96
PERTH	121	247	49.0	7.29	2.95
STRATFORD	143	321	44.5	6.79	2.11
KELSO	119	256	46.5	3.98	1.55
SOUTHWELL	86	183	47.0	2.59	1.41
DONCASTER	64	156	41.0	0.51	0.33
KEMPTON	71	169	42.0	-1.60	-0.95
ROSCOMMON	15	36	41.7	-0.87	-2.42
CARTMEL	53	127	41.7	-3.51	-2.76
CATTERICK	71	173	41.0	-5.43	-3.14
LEOPARDSTOWN	55	128	43.0	-4.35	-3.40
BELLEWSTOWN	10	24	41.7	-0.96	-3.99
CARLISLE	75	167	44.9	-6.76	-4.05

Course	Wins	Runners	%Win	Profit/loss(£)	Profit/ loss(%)
EXETER	83	187	44.4	-8.07	-4.32
LEICESTER	68	164	41.5	-7.15	-4.36
UTTOXETER	183	427	42.9	-20.88	-4.89
HEXHAM	114	261	43.7	-12.77	-4.89
GALWAY	17	41	41.5	-2.11	-5.16
TRALEE	13	33	39.4	-1.82	-5.52
NEWCASTLE	83	195	42.6	-11.32	-5.80
SEDGEFIELD	128	317	40.4	-19.30	-6.09
CHEPSTOW	114	272	41.9	-17.18	-6.32
LIMERICK	58	144	40.3	-9.15	-6.35
PUNCHESTOWN	61	161	37.9	-10.61	-6.59
DOWN ROYAL	37	99	37.4	-7.37	-7.45
MARKET RASEN	157	375	41.9	-29.72	-7.93
WARWICK	74	204	36.3	-18.45	-9.04
LUDLOW	123	305	40.3	-27.71	-9.09
CHELTENHM	72	196	36.7	-18.07	-9.22
TIPPERARY	21	51	41.2	-5.00	-9.80
FAKENHAM	47	114	41.2	-11.42	-10.02
NEWTON ABBOT	168	394	42.6	-41.93	-10.64
NAAS	25	66	37.9	-7.41	-11.22
FONTWELL	156	402	38.8	-55.25	-13.74
WETHERBY	113	278	40.6	-38.56	-13.87

Course	Wins	Runners	%Win	Profit/loss(£)	Profit/ loss(%)
AYR	79	178	44.4	-24.82	-13.95
WINCANTON	112	285	39.3	-43.02	-15.10
BANGOR	99	248	39.9	-39.43	-15.90
PLUMPTON	147	371	39.6	-61.37	-16.54
TRAMORE	23	77	29.9	-14.88	-19.33
THURLES	29	102	28.4	-20.80	-20.40
KILBEGGAN	23	68	33.8	-14.45	-21.25
SLIGO	16	50	32.0	-11.79	-23.57
FAIRYHOUSE	46	137	33.6	-33.27	-24.28
AINTREE	33	95	34.7	-23.17	-24.39
ASCOT	54	158	34.2	-42.54	-26.92
KILLARNEY	7	30	23.3	-17.08	-56.92

Why do favourites do better at some tracks than others?

It is anyone's guess as to why the favourite is profitable to back at these tracks and not at others. However, it is probably worth speculating on a few theories.

One hypothesis is that the on course punters at these tracks are particularly skilled and only bet horses that have a very good chance of winning. This is certainly possible because during the study period on-course punters largely determined the Starting Price returns. However, I find it hard to imagine that some racecourses attract more knowledgeable punters than others. There are though some people who subscribe to this theory.

A more plausible theory, in my opinion, is that the favourite does better at some courses than others because of some characteristic about the track. For instance, it is a statistical fact that the favourite has a relatively poor record on heavy going and certainly some racecourses are more likely to produce soft or heavy going than others due to the local climate and drainage.

One could go on speculating about the reasons as to why favourites enjoy more success at some tracks than at others. However, writing out a betting slip is not the same as writing an essay. There are no prizes for well-argued answers. It is winners that count, or more accurately in an era of betting exchanges, it is winners and losers that count.

Backing and laying the favourite

There is clear statistical evidence that favourites do well at some tracks and not at others. A profitable strategy would therefore be to back the favourite at the profitable tracks and to lay the favourite on the betting exchanges at the most unprofitable courses.

The problem for this strategy is that one only definitely knows the Starting Price favourite after the race. I know that it is possible to bet the Starting Price favourite in advance in some betting shops by writing out a slip that states that you want to back the SP favourite in certain races, but you would have to check with your local bookie about this.

The laying of the Starting Price favourite on the exchanges is more problematic. The only way to lay the favourite is to monitor all the bookmakers odds just prior to the start of the race and lay the horse that looks most likely to start as favourite. In most cases this should be pretty obvious, especially when there is an odds on favourite in the race but you might need to be more wary when there are a number of runners competing for outright favouritism.

My research definitely seems to suggest that there is a way to make a profit from backing and laying favourites at certain racecourses in non-handicap hurdles. However, one needs to carefully implement the strategy, especially when trying to lay the favourite on the betting exchanges.

7 THE BETTING MARKET

One of the biggest financial events of the twenty-first century was the credit crunch. That event challenged the view that financial markets are all knowing and the price always reflects all the information about the good or service (including financial products) being offered in the marketplace. That theory has a name. It is called the efficient market hypothesis. A big question for the punter in the twenty-first century is whether or not this theory is true in horse race betting markets today. This might just seem like an academic question but if it holds true in horse racing it means that the punter, in the long-run, can never hope to come out ahead. However, if it not true, or only partially true, then it means that punters can come out ahead.

Let me start with a bit more background on the efficient market hypothesis. In the early 1960s, Nobel Prize winning economist Eugene Fama put forth the theory of efficient markets called the Efficient Market Hypothesis. The theory is simple but powerful. It states that markets correctly price the value of a stock, or any other commodity, correctly. In other words, the price of a stock is not too high or too low. The price reflects all known information at a point in time.

The theory has three versions: strong form, semi-strong form and weak form. I'll focus on the strong and semi-strong forms of the theory. In strong form efficiency is where all information, public, personal and confidential, is instantly reflected in the prices. Therefore, punters are unable to achieve a competitive advantage. This degree of market efficiency implies that above average returns cannot be achieved regardless of a punters skill and access to information.

In the semi-strong version of the theory prices are also a reflection of publicly available information, and also move instantly. Since market prices already reflect public information, investors are unable to gain abnormal returns. However, this implies that punters with inside information i.e. information not publicly available (this could be gallop reports, stable information about the welfare of the horse, or unique form, speed or pace ratings that are not readily available to all punters) could gain an edge.

One key test of the theory is whether or not prices instantly reflect all information. In strong form the theory would say that markets are always efficient and provide continuously accurate assessments of prices, based on all the available information available at a particular point in time. This would imply that in the long-run you could never profit from betting on the horses because, even if you had a very good knowledge of the sport, all the information known about a horse is factored into the bookmakers prices at all times.

In semi-strong form the theory may only hold true for some of the time. For instance, the bookmakers opening odds on a horse may only reflect the assessment of the bookmaker about the horse's chance, and the views of a few market participants who bet on the race earlier in the day.

These odds may be higher or lower than the horse's true odds. It is only in the moments before the race is due to start, when all betters with a view on the race have participated in the market, that the odds reflect the true chance of the horse winning because this is the point when all the available information about the race is known and revealed to the market. All information is revealed at this point because if you had any inside information about a horse then you would seek to profit from it by entering the market and betting some hard cash before the race was about to start. In addition, every time the odds move out of line with the horse's true chances of winning then the most knowledgeable market participants will move in to profit from the overlays and underlays that the market might temporarily create, and the odds will move back towards the true odds of the horse winning. In this version of the theory the market is semi-efficient and creates the possibility for some players to win at the game because they are able to exploit these temporary inefficiencies.

I've tried to do some simple test of these two versions of the theory by comparing opening and final odds. My idea is that if you can make a profit by backing a horse at the final odds but only when the final odds are above the opening odds then this would suggest that the market is not strongly efficient. In this instance the final odds would contain no more information than the opening odds. Indeed, the opening odds would be a better guide than the final odds, which shouldn't be the case in the strong form version of the theory because the final odds should include all market information whereas the opening odds only include some information.

To test my idea, I needed lots of data. Fortunately I have a database of hundreds of thousands of races and it records the opening odds recorded by the market (sometimes called the 'first show'). These are the bookmaker's early odds. These odds typically include a very large over round because bookmakers know that their odds aren't accurate reflections of the true odds because they can't really predict which way punters will go on a particular horse. To insure themselves against the possibility that their odds line might be wrong they build in a margin of error by offering stingy opening odds. For instance, if a bookmaker thinks that a horse is really a 2-1 shot then they might be really stingy and offer the horse at odds of even-money, building in for themselves a big margin for error. To remove this bias, I normalised the opening odds by removing the over round to create a fair book, which means that the odds are a reflection of a horse's probability of winning and do not include a margin for the bookmaker. I also remove the over round from the final odds to create a fair comparison between the opening and final odds. The data for the final odds comes from the Betfair SP.

What did my analysis show? The result was clear. You would make a big loss betting horses whose final odds exceeded their opening odds. These horses didn't represent profitable overlays. Last year you would have lost more than 10 per cent following this strategy. This would suggest that the final odds do indeed contain more information than the opening odds. This supports the efficient market hypothesis.

I then re-ran the analysis but this time looked at handicap versus non-handicaps. My reasoning was that in handicap races the horses have more exposed form whereas in non-handicap races you have unexposed horses. In the latter inside information might be more important (which might only be available to the owner, trainer and stable staff), which would be reflected in the final odds but not necessarily in the opening odds. The opposite though might be true in races with horses with exposed form, when there is more information known about a horse prior to a race (such as in a handicap). In this instance the opening odds might be almost as good as the final odds.

My data suggested that this assessment might be about right in that the efficient market hypothesis looks to be less strong in races with exposed form because the losses from betting horses in handicap races that had higher final odds to opening odds were much lower than for non-handicap races.

This all suggests that punters generally might actually be better off – unless they are in receipt of inside information – by sticking to races in which there is plenty of information known about the runners. The efficient market hypothesis seems weaker in these circumstances. This would suggest that you might be more likely to be a profitable punter betting in handicaps or big non-handicap races, such as graded races over the jumps or Group or Listed races on the flat.

When is the best time to strike a value bet?

Picking winners is hard enough but to make a profit at the racing game you also need to place your bets at the best possible odds in order to maximise your chance of making a profit. If you consistently back at odds that are lower than the true chance of your selections winning then you will end up a losing punter in the end, even if you are brilliant at picking winners. In contrast if you consistently get odds greater than the true odds then, while you may not be the best tipster in the world, at the end of the day you will turn in a good profit. Most serious players know this. The troubling question for them is when to place a bet. Should they bet a selection early at the morning line odds or should they leave it and wait for the odds to lengthen? In this chapter I offer a few pointers.

Predicting the way a market will go is very difficult. I'm sure there are clever people out there, focussed on the financial markets, that have sophisticated statistical techniques to work out whether market prices are likely to rise or fall. For most punters this isn't an option and the decision is more about figuring out whether the price on offer, at any particular time, is a value one or not.

A lot of media attention focusses on the morning line odds. These are the odds that first appear about a horse at the start of the day. In some markets the volume of bets can be pretty thin and so the odds can be fairly volatile in the early stages, but by mid morning a reasonable picture of the morning odds is available. I've heard some punters argue that you will always be better off taking an early price. I can see this if you manage to get on at a guaranteed price, which means that even if you take an early price and the SP turns out to be greater than you will get the SP price instead. However, I'm not so sure that simply betting early gets you the best price. My argument would be that the early market makers (i.e. the bookmakers or exchange layers) are probably equally unsure about the winning chances of each horse in a race. They have made a judgement but I would reason that they are likely to be cautious and factor any uncertainty into the prices on offer. This would mean that, generally speaking, the morning line price is more likely than not to be a worse price than the SP i.e. the price available shortly before the close of the market.

To answer this question I've analysed over 800,000 horses and their Betfair prices in a 10 year period. The data records the Betfair Starting Price (BSP), which is basically the odds on the horse at the start of the race;

the Morning Line price which is the weighted average of all bets placed on a horse on the exchange in the period up to 11am. It also records the weighted average price of all bets placed up to the start of the race; the maximum price seen about a horse prior to the start and available to good money (i.e. to a 100 pounds); and the minimum or lowest price seen on the exchange, again to good money before the off. The results of my analysis are presented in Table A.

Table A: Different price types and accuracy in predicting winning strike rate, all race types, Great Britain

Price Type	Decimal Odds	Implied Win Probability	Actual Win Probability	Error	% Error
BSP	9.04	0.111	0.108	-0.002	-1.99%
Morning Line	8.34	0.120	0.108	0.011	10.56%
Pre Race Ave	8.39	0.119	0.108	0.011	9.90%
Pre Race Price Max	12.78	0.078	0.108	-0.030	-27.85%
Pre Race Price Min	9.03	0.111	0.108	0.002	2.11%

Table A shows the decimal odds of all winners over the study period at the BSP. It shows that the average BSP is 9.04 to 1. This represents a probability of 0.11. In other words the market thinks that horses at this price have an 11 per cent chance of winning. Interestingly the morning line price on the same set of winning horses is much lower at 8.34-1. This means that the morning line market thinks that horses at these odds have a 12 per cent of winning. The first conclusion therefore that can be drawn from this data is that you are better off betting just before the off at the starting price than betting at the early morning price because the odds of reward are better at the SP. The early bird doesn't catch the worm...or so it would appear.

The interesting thing to note about the data in Table A is that the average price of all bets placed on winners before the race is 8.38. Again this is lower than the BSP but slightly better than the morning line price. This suggests that market makers (the layers) are fairly risk averse in their initial offerings in the morning, but then prices will be pushed out by market forces.

Students of the efficient market hypothesis will also note that the odds tend to converge towards the true or actual probabilities of winning. For instance, the BSP gives a probability of 11.1 per cent. This is very close to the actual win probability of 10.8%, an error of just under 2 per cent. The morning line odds suggest a win probability of 12 per cent, which is very different from the actual rate of 10.8%. This represents an error of more than 10 per cent. These calculations don't factor in commission on winning bets to the exchange and so in both instances you wouldn't make money, but you would lose a lot less simply backing at the SP compared to taking the morning line price. The conclusion here is that the final odds prior to the off are pretty accurate and reflect the true probabilities, probably due to all information being taken into account about the runners at this point, with all inside information being revealed to the market just before the off.

One erroneous conclusion from this data would be to think that you can't make money betting on the gee gees. You could believe this if you just compare the BSP to the actual win probabilities. The fact that they are so closely aligned could suggest that you can never beat the market. However, the data suggests that this may be wrong. The average pre race maximum price on all winners before the off was as high as 12.78. This is 3.74 points higher than the BSP, or a massive 41 per cent. The minimum pre-race price was just under the BSP. This clearly shows that it may not be the early bird that catches the worm but instead it is the punter who knows value when he sees it. Basically you would make a small fortune if you could work out ahead of the market the true odds of a horse winning, and then back the horse when the odds move above the true odds. In that way you would always make a value bet. Some professional punters seem to have that skill, and that is why they make money and others do not.

In summary, to be a profitable punter in the twenty-first century you need to have an appreciation for how markets work, and their level of accuracy at various time points. Horse race betting markets would appear to fairly efficient in that the final odds settle on the true odds. However, this is not the case at all times. The prices are often moving above the true odds. The key to success is to capture the value price when it appears. The early bird may therefore be the one that catches the worm. The late riser might have already missed the market value.

Creating an odds line for turf flat racing

The basic rationale is that to make serious money betting you need to be able to identify value bets. Simply picking winners will not be enough to make money in the long run. However, while people talk about making 'value' bets and assessing 'value' what are they talking about?

To assess 'value' properly you basically need to consider all the information in the form book. and work out what you think are the true chances of a horse winning a race. The next step is then to compare your assessment of the true odds with that of a bookmaker. If they offer better odds than your assessment then you have identified a value bet. This is what is called creating an odds line. For instance, your odds line might suggest that a particular horse is a 5 to 4 shot but the bookmakers have it chalked up at 5 to 1. The horse is clearly value and one would want to lump on at those odds. Conversely if you think a 5-4 shot should really be priced up at 5-1 then you have a great opportunity to lay the horse at odds below what you estimate to be its true chance of winning. However, this all depends on how good your original method was at estimating the true probability of a horse winning, and in identifying the true odds.

A system that overestimated a horses chance of winning would identify plenty of value bets but you would end up losing in the long run because the bookmakers odds would more accurately reflect the true odds. In other words you would think that you were backing genuine 5 to 4 shots but later find your selections were winning at the frequency you would expect of horses priced at 5 to 1. In other words you would be expecting to record a strike rate of 44 per cent on your bets but ended up with just 17%. The first and most important thing is therefore to create a system that accurately reflects a horse's true odds of winning. This is easier said than done. Some people have a natural instinct for this sort of thing, whereas others prefer a more technical approach. I follow the latter.

In this Chapter I am going to take you through the four steps you would need to cover to produce a fairly reliable odds line for flat turf handicaps.

In order to implement the method you will need some familiarity with Microsoft EXCEL or possess a scientific calculator. You will also need access to the Racing Post newspaper or members only website.

Step 1

Let us first create a system that generates an accurate odds line. There are two approaches that could be taken here. One is to produce what is termed a *fundamental* system. This is one where you create an odds line from a system based on *only* form factors. This sounds like the right approach but these types of system can take years of research to produce. A quicker way to developing an odds line is to produce a system that incorporates the bookies odds into a fundamental system to create an assessment of the horses accurate or fair odds.

For clarity I should say that when I refer to accurate or fair odds I mean the true probability of a horse winning. Thus if a horse is estimated to have accurate or true odds of 2 to 1 it has a 33 per cent chance of winning because for every three horses priced at these odds two horses would be expected to lose and one would be expected to win. This works out as a probability of 33 per cent (2/1 = 1/3 = 0.33 or 33%). Decimal odds make this easier as a horse with a 33% chance of winning has decimal odds of

3:1 (1/3).

Let us now get down to building the system on which we will base our odds line. For the purposes of this C I have produced a simple system designed to produce accurate odds for turf flat handicaps.

The system I have created is based on the following factors:

1. Weight carried (in pounds); with horses carrying more weight having a reduced chance of winning.

2. The Racing Post Rating or RPR earned by the horse in its last race, with the higher the rating the better the horses chance.

3. The Racing Post Top Speed rating or TS earned by the horse in its last race, with the higher the rating the better the horses chance.

4. The first show or opening odds of the horse (in decimal odds). This is the price that the horse was when the betting market opened. The shorter the odds the more likely the horse will win.

You will note that the system has only four factors, with one of them being the First show price recorded by bookmakers (not the Exchange price). How can this simple system possibly estimate a horse's true odds of winning? Well, the key is in the weighting of the variables. This is the most crucial part of the whole exercise and can only be accurately estimated by in depth research. For present purposes we will ignore this. You will just have to take it on trust that the variables are weighted appropriately.

The weightings are as follows:

x1	=	TS1	*.003
x2	=	RPR1	*.007
x3	=	Weight (lbs)	*-.004
x4	=	1st show odds (decimal)	*-.091

Note: '' means multiplied by the weighting factor.*

Now let us consider an example picked from my database at random from the last decade.

Horse	**SP**	**TS**	**RPR**	**Weight (lbs)**	**1st odds**
Kingswinford	17	56	73	128	19.0
Local Singer	13	63	65	128	11.0
Seeking Magic	1.5	85	88	133	1.7
Roodee queen	9.5	44	69	128	5.5
Perfect Pastime	5.5	56	84	132	6.5

Horse	**x1**	**x2**	**x3**	**x4**	**sum**	**p**	**sum p**	**Norm p**	**fair sp**
Kingswinford	0.2	0.5	-0.5	-1.7	-1.6	0.2	3.2	0.1	15.3
Local Singer	0.2	0.5	-0.5	-1.0	-0.9	0.4	3.2	0.1	7.6
Seeking Magic	0.3	0.6	-0.5	-0.2	0.2	1.2	3.2	0.4	2.7
Roodee queen	0.1	0.5	-0.5	-0.5	-0.4	0.7	3.2	0.2	4.8
Perfect Pastime	0.2	0.6	-0.5	-0.6	-0.4	0.7	3.2	0.2	4.6

If you weight all the variables correctly and add up x1+x2+x3+x4 for Seeking Magic you get a sum (x sum) of 0.2. What does this mean? At this stage not a lot but we need to move to Step 2. This is when you will really need your calculator or access to Microsoft EXCEL.

Step 2

This is when things get a bit technical and we have some nasty maths to get through, but this is a necessary evil if we are to turn our system into an odds line.

In the next part of the calculation we need to take the total score of 0.2 and enter it into the following formula in MICROSOFT EXCEL:

=EXP(x_sum)

In the example if you enter exp(0.2) into an EXCEL spreadsheet you should get a figure of around 1.2.

Does this now mean that we have the horse's odds of winning? Not quite. But we are nearly there.

Step 3

In order to work out its true odds of winning this particular race we need to work out what is called the *normalised* odds. These are the odds that take into account the level of within race competition.

The normalised probabilities can be calculated by simply adding the scores (denoted by p in our table) of all the horses together. For the example race when you sum all the p values together for all he horses you get a total of 3.2 (sum_p)

Step 4

To get the fair decimal odds we now simply take the p value for each horse and divide it by sum_p. For Seeking Magic 1.2/3.2= 0.4. This means that the horse has a 40% chance of winning. To convert this to decimal odds you simply compute 1/0.4=2.7.

You now repeat this process for every runner in the race and you then have a complete set of fair odds.

Our example odds line, once complete, makes for interesting reading.

Seeking Magic is the bookmakers favourite but looks shocking value. The bookies SP for this horse is 1-2 or 1.5 in decimal odds. Many punters are clearly prepared to back this horse at the odds-on in this five horse race. However, armed with our odds line we can clean out these punters pockets because we know that the horses true chance or true odds is nothing like 1-2. Our odds line actually makes Seeking Magic odds-against at decimal odds of 2.7.

Given that the odds-on favourite is such poor value in a five runner race there now looks to be value in every other runner. Incidentally the race was won by Kingswinford at decimal odds of 17-1, but our system rated it better value than that.

In summary, I've tried to explain how an odds line can be created from a system. Some aspects are a bit technical but once you start to practice creating your own odds lines you will soon find that things become easier, and you can start adding some additional variables and create your own weightings for each factor.

What is arbitrage?

As discussed previously, one of the biggest changes this century for the punter was the advent of the betting exchanges. This allowed punters to back and lay horses in the exchange. In other words the punter could be a trader and play the odds to make a profit regardless of the race outcome, The method for doing this is called arbitrage.

Basically, the idea behind arbitrage is to buy at a low price and sell at a high one. The application in horse racing (or any other betting proposition) is to Lay at low odds and Back at at high odds. Naturally, things are a bit more complicated than that, and one of the issues is how much money to risk when backing and laying.

Let's walk through an example. Let's say that you back a horse to a stake of £100 at 3.00 (at decimal odds or 2-1 at bookmaker odds) and let's say you then lay the horse at 2.00, again for a stake of £100. If the horse wins, the profit on your win bet is £200 and the loss on your lay bet is £100 - you've gained a net profit of £100. If the horse loses, the loss on your win bet is £100 and the profit on your lay is £100 - you haven't lost anything, but you haven't gained anything either.

For many people this is perfectly satisfactory - after all you've had the chance to gain £100 for zero risk. However, suppose in the foregoing example you had, as previously, backed the horse to a stake of £100 at 3.0, but then, when the horse was available to lay at 2.0 you had layed it for a stake of £150. Now, if the horse wins, the profit on your win bet is again £200 but the loss on your lay bet is £150. Your net profit is reduced to £50. BUT, If the horse loses, the loss on your win bet is £100 but the profit on your lay bet is £150 - a net profit of £50. In other words you make the same net profit whether the horse wins or loses.

Now that was an easy example using nice round figures, but suppose you've backed the horse to a £100 stake at 2.73 and you have the opportunity to lay it at 1.9. How much should your Lay stake be to equalise your profit whether the horse wins or loses? Well, there's a formula:

Lay Stake = Back Stake * Back Odds / Lay Odds

In the example above, to equalise your profits whether the horse wins or loses, your lay stake should be:

100 * 2.73 / 1.9 = £ 143.68

Therefore your net profit, whether the horse wins or loses, will be £43.68. Similarly, if you've already layed a horse (e.g. £100 at 2.7), but now see an opportunity to back it at longer odds (e.g. 3.3):

Back Stake = Lay Stake * Lay Odds / Back Odds

e.g: 100 * 2.7 / 3.3 = £81.82 for a guaranteed profit of £18.18

How to win and lose a fortune: using the Kelly Criterion in practice

Successful gamblers have two distinct advantages over their peers. They know when the odds are stacked in their favour and they know how much to bet in order to maximise their advantage. For example, Bill Benter who leads the most successful Hong Kong betting syndicate wins around $20m per year because he has worked out the true odds of a horse winning a race and uses that information to determine how much to bet. Regarding the latter Benter, like many other sophisticated punters, uses a mathematical formula called the Kelly Criterion to maximise his profits.

The Kelly criterion is a formula that tells a gambler how much of their betting bank to bet on each round of a profitable gamble so as to maximise the growth rate of their wealth. The formula has been shown to work. For example, in a paper written in 1994 Bill Benter explained how he had used the Kelly formula to win several times his initial wealth in a sequence of around 2,500 horse races. Not bad! Other famous gamblers and investors like Edward Thorp used Kelly when counting cards at blackjack. The claim has also been made that well-known successful investors including Warren Buffett and Bill Gross also use Kelly methods.

What is this magic Kelly Formula? The full details are explained by the formula's inventor J.L.Kelly, in his seminal paper *A New Interpretation of Information Rate* (Bell System Technical Journal, 35, 917-926). However, I'm no mathematician and much of the paper makes little sense to me. However, I've poured over the details in the paper, and those revealed in other more accessible papers and articles, and from my understanding the formula is this:

$$f = (p \, . \, b - (1-p)) / b$$

Where f is the proportion of your bankroll to bet on each event; p is your true probability of winning on the bet; and b is the decimal odds on the bet (e.g. an even money pay-off would be expressed as 2.0), which is basically your potential pay-off on the bet (the dot between the p and the b simply means multiply p by b).

The formula is probably best explained with an example. Imagine you have a betting bank of £100 and you have a situation whereby a horse in priced at decimal odds of 3.5 (b) but you know the true probability of winning the wager is 33 per cent (p). If you plug these numbers into the formula above then you should get the figure 0.06 (6 per cent). This means that Kelly is telling you to bet 6 per cent of your total betting bank or £6 out of your initial £100. If you bet more than this then, over a large series of bets, you will eventually lose your wealth despite having the probabilities in your favour. If you bet less then you will not maximise your potential profit.

This all seems pretty simple, and provided that you know your probability of success (BIG 'if'), you don't even have to do the maths as there are plenty of online staking calculators that will do the number crunching for you. However, as Kelly's original paper demonstrates, the criterion is only valid when the situation is played many times over, with the same probability of winning or losing each time, and the same payout ratio. In other words Kelly should ensure that you maximise your betting wealth in the long-run, but in the long-run we are all dead. In reality the fates might decide that you lose in your first dozen bets or so. At that point the Kelly formula will have pretty much blown away all your betting capital. To avoid this situation many users of the Kelly formula prefer to bet only a fraction of the full Kelly wager i.e. someone betting to half-Kelly would bet 3 per cent of their bank roll in our example and someone betting to one-quarter Kelly would be betting just 1.5 per cent. A careful reading of one of Bill Benter's papers on his Hong Kong betting syndicate reveals that painful experience taught him and his colleagues that betting to full Kelly stakes wasn't advisable. Indeed it is known that in his early days Benter lost pretty much all the syndicates betting capital.

The question that interests me is therefore not whether or not Kelly is a good investment formula – that is pretty much proven by the mathematicians and successful practitioners – but what fraction of Kelly should one bet? Should it be to the full Kelly percentage or to some other fraction?

Let me give you an illustration by looking at how Kelly performs on one of my systems. I won't go into the details of the system itself but basically it helps me create an odds lines for each and every horse in a race i.e. it provides an estimate of what I think are the true odds or probabilities of success for each contender. I can then compare my estimates to the odds on offer to see if I have a value bet.

The system only selects one horse in each race, provided that it is a value bet. All the selections are in handicaps, and so I'm betting in races with big fields. The random probability of any horse winning in races with big fields is obviously lower than in races with smaller field sizes. However, the overall strike rate of the system is around 20 per cent since over a five year period. The important thing to note is that to a simple level stake bet the system has shown a profit of around 10 per cent on turnover in each and every year over the study period. Sometimes it has been a bit less and sometimes it has been a bit more than 10 per cent but overall it looks to be a reliable system that shows a modest profit at level stakes.

Can the full Kelly formula boost profits for this system? The short answer is no. I found that Kelly made huge bets on selections that looked to have a big edge, but if a few of these lost in a sequence then the betting bank was quickly exhausted. In my simulation I started with £1000. In around a dozen bets Kelly had increased the bank to £2,500. At this point you would have thought that the Kelly formula was the key to the mint but Kelly continued with its preference for big wagers and placed 22 per cent of the entire bank roll on one 5-2 shot. That lost but on bet 30 Kelly decided to stake over half the remaining bank roll on an odds-on shot that duly lost. This took the bank down to under half it's original level.

Full Kelly was a roller-coaster and by bet 44 the bank was right back up to round £1,400, but at bet 51 Kelly went all out for an 8-11 shot and staked 51 per cent of the available bank on that one horse. That went down and there then followed a losing run that saw just 1 winner in the next 15 bets. The betting bank was now down to just a £100. Kelly though managed to bring it back up again to over £300 by bet 93.

A desperate losing run of 12 losers on the bounce during which Kelly decided to go 10% and 20% bets saw the bank drain to virtually nothing. Kelly managed to get it up again after a winning run but by that point the bank was too small to give me any chance of getting back the original £1000. At around bet 300 the entire bank was exhausted but for a few pence.

Betting to full Kelly stakes was clearly too bold for my system. The problem seems to be that the system has losing runs because it has a low strike rate and that full Kelly is too bold with its stakes. Of course this could be due to the system being inaccurate in its assessment of the true winning probabilities, causing Kelly to bet too much than desired. Would though a more cautious Kelly strategy avoid these problems?

This time I repeated the simulation on the same sample of results but this time bet only to ¼ Kelly stakes to stop Kelly betting my shirt on a single selection. The results are fascinating. There wasn't the spectacular start like under fully Kelly but the bank was in credit. However, it then had to navigate those two big losing runs than I described above. The bank fell to a low of just over £700 by bet 195. However, while losing a third of ones betting capital isn't great this wasn't the disaster we had when betting to full Kelly. At this stage under full Kelly the bank was pretty much empty.

At bet 224 the bank grew to over £2,000. The next stage was a bit choppy but by bet 338 the bank was now over three grand! The ride was then still a bit rough but the capital was always well above £1,500 at its lowest and then rose so that by bet 552 the bank was over £6,000! Amazing. We had taken a profit of over 5 grand, although we had to be confident given the roller coaster to get there. At bet number 700 the bank was up to over 9 grand! There were still downward swings but the overall profile was a rising one. Kelly is clearly a genius! At bet 726 the bank hit the 10 grand mark.

The system then went crazy and hit a big winning run, with Kelly piling on the cash. This was a lucky run on the same scale as the losing runs we had experienced before. The bank was now £60,000 at bet 926. Incredible. However, the gods of fate again intervened. The bank hovered around 60k to 50k for a long period before a series of long losing runs again caused a major crash. In the end the bank was down to around £4,500 at the end of the simulation period. The results had clearly been much better than under full Kelly but I'd challenge anyone to think that having £60k at one point and £4.5k at the end of the day was totally successful!

Nevertheless the bank was clearly much bigger than the original £1,000, and much bigger than it would have been under level stakes.

More cautious Kelly strategies were then tested. The upswings and downswing's could be moderated by employing 1/8th and 1/16th Kelly strategies and the final balances were around £5,500 and £6,000 under these respective strategies.

The above simulations show that full Kelly doesn't seem to work when betting on outcomes with a low probability of success. The losing runs are often long and if Kelly bets to high stakes then the bank quickly becomes exhausted. The flip side is that full Kelly will grow the bank roll more quickly during a winning run than the alternatives.

I then started to think about using Kelly but trying to reduce the losing runs. I studied the research on the Kelly formula and one line in a book I read said that I was doing it all wrong. I should be betting ALL the value bets in the race and making bets according to a variant of the Kelly formula which basically treats a race as one big bet, and stakes are placed on each horse according to the value they represent. However, curiously the formula may tell you to bet a horse that is not great value but has a high probability of winning as a 'saver'. Clever stuff.

The formula for multiple bets on the same race is a bit involved. I've worked through the maths myself and then found this online calculator that does all the work for you (see www.sportsbookreview.com/picks/tools/kelly-calculator/). It is U.S based calculator but you can plug in decimal odds like those displayed on Betfair and other betting exchanges and it will work the stakes for you.

To give you an idea about how the multi bet strategy works in practice consider the Class 5 ‘Introducing RacingTV Handicap Hurdle’ at Musselburgh on Sunday 10th March. This race featured a number of horses that had dubious levels of form as is often the case in low grade races.

My odds line had St George's Oval as the favourite at decimal odds of 7.34. His Betfair price 15 minutes before the race was 8.6. He was a value bet on my book. However, I didn’t give much of a chance to the favourite Splash The Cash or the second favourite Danceintothelight. Among other negatives, Slash The Cash had posted a best Racing Post Rating of 97 but had top weight . Danceintothelight had a similar sort of rating but was a 12 year-old and on the decline. Both horses ran well below their BHA rating the last time they ran. Frame Rate had similar ratings but was 27 to 1 and had a trainer who was in red hot form. Therefore the favourite and second favourite had to rate as longer shots than the market suggested. If this was true then this made a fair few of the other runners as value bets.

The Table below shows you the stake suggested by Kelly to a £100 bankroll using a multi bet strategy. Any errors are my own as I used my own calculations for sizing the bets on this race (also note that I also slightly increase the odds in my odds line to account for commission and error).

Horse	Odds Line	Price	Return	Bet Size	Stake	Return
Country Delights	15.07	230	£15.26	6.46%	£6.46	£1,479.58
Solway Lark	22.4	95	£4.24	4.04%	£4.04	£379.90
Frame Rate	10.98	27	£2.46	7.62%	£7.62	£198.12
Cadore	58.24	120	£2.06	1.38%	£1.38	£164.50
Max Liebermann	14.12	23	£1.63	5.34%	£5.34	£117.39

Horse	Odds Line	Price	Return	Bet Size	Stake	Return
Reivers Lodge	22.43	30	£1.34	3.12%	£3.12	£90.46
Betancourt	10.01	13	£1.30	6.90%	£6.90	£82.80
St George's Oval	7.34	8.6	£1.17	8.95%	£8.95	£68.05
Avondhu Pearl	10.12	11	£1.09	6.23%	£6.23	£62.30
Dance Of Fire	9.79	9.4	£0.96	5.94%	£5.94	£49.91
Dizoard	19.82	13.5	£0.68	2.07%	£2.07	£25.88
Rioja Day	18.97	11.5	£0.61	1.78%	£1.78	£18.68
Splash The Cash	21.91	5.1	£0.23	-3.31%		
Danceintothelight	31.38	7	£0.22	-2.55%		

Based on my tissue prices a bet could be placed on most of the runners. From a bank of £100 (which keeps the maths simple) the Kelly multi bet formula suggested that a stake of £60 was justified. Dance of Fire, Dizoard and Rioja Day would act as 'savers' in that they would be losers in my book but not disasters. The disasters would be Splash the Cash and Danceinthelight who we strongly opposed. Everything else would be a winner.

In the event Frame Rate was the winner at 27-1. This horse was a very good value bet on my tissue price. At a stake of £7.62 the return on the winner paid a profit of £198.12, and only the rags Solway Lark and Country Delights would have offered bigger returns.

In summary, betting more than one horse in a race can be very good value if you have a good odds line, and especially when you can identify false favourites. When used correctly, the Kelly formula can help you allocate you bets among the value bets to help maximise the long-run return on your capital.

8 BETTING SYSTEMS

Ever since I first encountered a computer in the early 1980s I wondered whether it could be utilised to implement automated betting systems. In my fantasy I would use information from a computerised form database to research and develop profitable systems. My PC would then analyse the database for the forthcoming days racing and work out selections based on my systems. It would then place bets on the selections, according to my own staking formula and at the best available prices. The human element would therefore be removed from the betting process and with it the room for error. It would also take considerable effort out of the betting process and allow me to relax and enjoy my winnings, and dream up new systems and strategies.

This way of betting may have been a fantasy in the 1980s but in the twenty-first century it is now a reality. Even with intermediate computer skills you can now develop your own automated systems, or purchase software that will do it for you. The advent of the Betfair API now also makes it possible to feed in thousands of bets into the exchange based on your own rules.

However, while the technology is now in place to automate betting systems there is one fundamental factor that has not changed. You still need to develop profitable betting systems. This is an ongoing process because a betting system will not work forever. This has always been true because betting systems lose their edge when more and more people find out the same angle. This turns a profitable system into a losing one because the value that the system exploited gradually gets eroded.

In the twenty-first century the shelf life of systems seems to be getting shorter. I don't know for certain why this is the case but I suspect that the advent of computerised form databases and online form books have made it easier for people to research systems and find winning angles. This doesn't mean that you cannot find your own winning systems, and I've found some angles that have defied the trend and stayed profitable for several years. It does though mean that you have to work a little bit harder to stay ahead of the pack, and keep coming up with new ideas for systems. In the pages that follow I've probably shot myself in the foot by giving away some of my system ideas but I'm working on the assumption that not many people will be reading this book (thank you by the way!), and by the time you read this I will have come up with some new angles to exploit! I do hope that the systems that follow spark your own ideas because if you are a geek like me then you will find that researching and developing betting systems is fun, and can be very profitable.

The money horse system

A good way to become a successful punter is to play a portfolio of systems. This has worked for me down the years, and I know that this is an approach favoured by a number of other serious players. The concept is very simple but has a good statistical rationale behind it, and adopts the same approach as any successful investor in the financial markets.

The strategy is basically to develop a whole range of betting systems and then to play them at the same time. Provided a system has been well researched and has proved to be successful in a trial period then it should be added to one's system portfolio.

In playing a whole range of different systems the punter effectively spreads his or her risk, provided that the portfolio is big enough, and diverse enough in its range of strategies. I'll illustrate what I mean with an example from my own experience. A number of years ago I developed a system that I thought was excellent and indeed profits had been very good. The system was so effective that I was betting solely using that one system and had invested all of my betting capital on it. This worked for a while but then something happened that meant that the system didn't work any more and it lost me a heap of cash. I managed to pull the plug before it sent me into the red but a lesson was learnt the hard way: never invest all your betting capital in just one idea. The same principle is used by city traders. They don't put all of their eggs in one basket. They spread their capital around on a whole number of different trades: They might not all come off but if one makes a loss on one system then the rest of the portfolio should be able to compensate and keep the overall fund in profit.

The same approach can work well for systems punters. You just need to develop a portfolio of decent systems. You should keep them all under constant review and cull any that no longer appear to be profitable, and replace them with new systems. It is also a good idea to develop systems that don't cut across one another. For instance, don't have a number of systems all targeting two-year olds or handicaps etc. or otherwise you will end up betting against yourself in the target races.

The difficult bit is coming up with good systems. You also want a range of systems that have different levels of risk. Your portfolio should have a mix of high risk and low risk strategies, with more low risk plays in the portfolio so that if the high risk strategy goes belly up it won't sink the whole portfolio.

Another good principle to follow is not to develop systems that involve too many factors. These types of plays will inevitably start to overlap with the factors you are using in other systems. You therefore might think that you are running a portfolio of systems but in reality you are riding on just a few factors that are common to all the systems you are using. This isn't a good way to manage your risks. You should aim for diversity in your systems, so that each works on a different angle and captures a unique piece of information. The best way to do this is to keep your system simple so that you can understand how they all work together, and where they overlap.

One simple system is to follow what I call 'money horses'. The money horse system looks very basic but has a decent rationale behind it. The rules of the system are to back every horse that was a beaten favourite on its last run but only if it opens in the betting market as the favourite. The logic here is that for a horse to be sent off as favourite in its previous race someone must have had confidence in it. These might be connections or form experts.

Backing beaten favourites blindly though isn't a winning strategy. In fact it makes a big fat loss. The logic of the 'money horse' system is that if a horse attracted enough money to make it start favourite on its last outing but got beaten then someone got their fingers burnt. Therefore if the horse again opens as the favourite in its next race then connections might be looking to get their money back, and have moved in again to recoup their losses. An alternative explanation is that the horse was good enough to start favourite last time but experienced bad luck. It is starting favourite again because it still looks good enough to win provided that bad luck doesn't strike again.

There are some important details to consider before implementing the system., The definition of a beaten favourite should be based on the bookmakers starting price. This is how the newspapers define a beaten favourite in their form guides. The horse in question will appear with a 'BF' next to its name to denote that it started as the bookies favourite in its last race but didn't win. You then back these horses provided that the horse opens in the betting as the favourite once again. Favourites in this case are horses that are favourite according to the bookmakers opening odds, as reported by the starting price reporters at the track. These odds represent the on-course bookies opening shows for the race. They convey a heap of information in that they represent all the bets that have been placed on the race during the rest of the day and will include bets placed in betting shops. They will also include information about how the bookies think the market will work out.

The use of the opening bookmaker odds in this system also has a practical advantage. The opening odds usually appear 10 minutes before the scheduled off time for a race. This gives plenty of time to work out the selection of the race and to get a bet on at the best possible price.

You may be thinking that this all sounds very simple but requires the system operator to be on the track to identify the opening odds on each horse. Certainly you can play this system on-course but you can also play it in your local bookie as the first shows on-course are always reported back. You can also get live odds online from a variety of different sources, such as the Sporting Life website. This has live shows for all UK and Irish racing and being online allows one then to determine the best odds at which to back the selection once the first show has been received. Getting the best odds on system selections is also very simple. One simply bets every selection at a price higher than the bookmakers opening show.

My data on this system shows that in a five year period a modest but useful profit was generated. This was based on betting beaten favourites when they open in the betting as favourite, and then backing them at odds longer than their opening price in the minutes before the start of the race. For analysis purposes I have assumed that a bet would be made when the Betfair Starting Price was higher than the bookmakers opening show on the selection. My results show that you would have made 3,400 selections and would have had 990 winners. This represents a healthy strike rate of 29 per cent. In terms of the bottom line, rate of return was around 10 per cent without commission and about 6 per cent with commission paid at 5 per cent on all winning returns. This certainly isn't a get rich quick scheme but it might be a useful system to add to your portfolio.

Is betting horses to place a winning system?

Picking winners is hard. Is it easier and more profitable to back horses to place? The answer must obviously be "yes" but if you bet horses to place then your returns per bet will be lower because the odds to place will be much lower than the win odds. You therefore need to pick of lot of horses to place in order to make a profit. This might be just as hard or harder than picking winners!

What do the statistics tell us? My research over the last nine months shows that if you bet every forecast favourite in the Racing Post newspaper to place on the exchanges then you would win just a shade under 60 per cent of all your bets. That is a great strike rate, and if you don't like losing runs then this statistic will appeal. The statistic though that you won't like is that if you bet every forecast favourite to place at the Betfair place starting price then you would make a small loss before commission, but a loss of around 3 per cent after the standard five per cent commission. Over a large number of bets that adds up to a sizeable amount of money lost. Ouch!

A different approach might be to bet for a place only those forecast favourites that are odds-on. This isn't a bad idea. My data shows that around 87 per cent of forecast odds-on favourites place. This actually makes a profit of just over one per cent after commission to the exchange. This is hardly worth the bother given the risk of one or two results going the wrong way and turning a profit into a loss, but it is worth noting.

Betting forecast odds-on favourites to place might be something on which we can build. Betting extreme odds-on favourites to place might be one way to go. The strategy would be to bet all odds-on favourites that are shorter than 1-2 in the betting forecast. Following this strategy in my sample of data suggests that you would return a profit of 5 per cent after commission. However, over nine months you would only have made 117 wagers, with 112 of the selections being successfully placed in the place exchange market, a 96 per cent strike rate. You could try to apply more filters to this system to try to weed out false odds-on favourites to increase the rate of return further but you would end up being so selective that you would hardly make any bets during the average season. For example this method has a 100 per cent success rate in chases ,but restricting your bets to chasers would only yield 17 bets in nine months.

Building on the above strategy if you bet every forecast odds-on favourite in chases for a place then, even after commission, you would earn a rate of return of over 12 per cent, recording a success rate of just over 90 per cent. The number of selections would be small but you would make around 80 bets over a nine month period following this strategy.

Another strategy might be to use place betting only on horses that are good value to place. One common strategy for place betting is to bet the clear second favourite to place when the favourite is odds-on. I'm sceptical about this one when using the betting exchange place betting market because we have seen that forecast odds-on favourites are highly likely to place, which means that there isn't much room in the winners enclosure for the the other horses. My data suggests that this strategy generates a lot of selections but after commission the profit is less than two per cent. It though is interesting that the record of second favourites to place is much poorer in chases than in hurdle or flat races.

I'm not sure why you get this result other than that in these chase races the second favourite might be the second favourite because they are sketchy jumpers and may therefore not place because they fall or make mistakes. It might also be the case that in chase races, because the odds-on favourite is highly likely to place, the second favourite is competing for the remaining one or two place spots. In contrast in hurdle and flat races the second favourite has a good place record when the favourite is odds-on. In these races the second favourite is placed around 60 per cent of the time and returns a profit of over five per cent after commission.

In terms of a system for place betting the following rules might produce a profit going forward:

- Bet the forecast favourite in a chase race to place when the forecast odds are less than even money;

- Bet the clear forecast second favourite (i.e. not ties for second favourite) in all hurdles and flat races when the favourite is odds-on.

Following these simple rules would yield a profit of just over 6 per cent after paying a 5 per cent commission on all winning bets. You would be successful around 63 per cent of the time. Not a fortune but not a bad little system.

Can you score with penalties?

According to the very useful "Guide to handicapping" published by the British Horse Racing Authority the essence of handicapping is:

> *"...that the weight a horse carries ultimately affects the speed at which it can gallop. A handicap is a race where each horse is set to carry a weight, allocated according to the horse's ability, in an attempt to equalise every horse's chance of winning. Every time a horse runs in a race the performance is analysed by the 'Handicapper' and the horse (depending on various qualifying criteria) is allocated a rating. Every case is judged on its individual merits with the Handicapper taking into account all*

the pertinent variables such as the weight the horse carried in relation to other runners, the race distance, the ground, the draw (if a Flat race), the finishing margins between runners, the pace at which the race was run, the strength of the current form of the runners, and whether any incidents occurred that could have impeded one or more of the runners or exaggerated a horse's performance. The ratings are expressed in imperial pounds and are based on the concept that all horses can be assessed on a numerical scale that enables their ability as a racehorse to be compared to others".

Horse's ratings are assessed once a week by the official handicappers of the British Horse Racing Authority (BHA). This creates an opportunity for the wily trainer because it is possible for a horse to race again off the same official handicap rating within seven days. It is perfectly possible that a trainer could exploit a horses ratings and get two or three wins in a week out of the horse because it is so well handicapped. To level out this advantage the BHA require a horse to run under a penalty three, five or seven pounds to cancel out any advantage that they might have. However, if a trainer thinks the horses ratings is going to go up by a lot more than seven pounds because it is improving and in its last race it won with plenty in hand then they will still exploit the advantage and run again even though the horse will have a penalty to carry.

Sir Mark Prescott, who regularly manages to get his horses to rattle up long winning sequences due to this rule, is a master of exploiting a horses handicap mark and his horses on the flat always need plenty of respect if running under a penalty. There are also a number of jump trainers that are also excellent at winning races with horses running under a penalty.

There aren't that many horses that run under a penalty. In my analysis over a four year period there were only about 1,200 horses that carried a penalty in National Hunt races. They do though have a high strike rate. The average win rate of horses carrying a penalty in handicap races over the jumps is about 29 per cent based in my research. This is considerably higher than if you just picked a horse in each race at random. Following that method you would pick around nine winners in every hundred bets. However, some trainers look to do significantly better than others with their penalty carriers, and some record very high strike rates.

I've done plenty of research in this area and there are profits to be had by following certain trainers that have runners carrying a penalty. In terms of my analysis, in order to keep samples high enough, I excluded trainers that had fewer than six runners carrying a penalty. This reduces the list of trainers to under 50 (see below)

Strike rate of trainers with horses carrying a penalty

Trainer	Runners	Wins	Strike rate (%)
David Bridgwater	15	11	73%
Dan Skelton	19	10	53%
Johnny Farrelly	12	6	50%
Anthony Honeyball	19	9	47%
Jonjo ONeill	34	15	44%
Jennie Candlish	7	3	43%

Trainer	Runners	Wins	Strike rate (%)
Micky Hammond	7	3	43%
Philip Hobbs	7	3	43%
Jim Best	12	5	42%
Sue Smith	12	5	42%
Jeremy Scott	10	4	40%
Ian Williams	16	6	38%
Bernard Llewellyn	8	3	38%
David Dennis	11	4	36%
Neil King	17	6	35%
Neil Mulholland	29	10	34%
Venetia Williams	48	16	33%
Evan Williams	36	12	33%
Tony Carroll	12	4	33%
Charlie Longsdon	9	3	33%
Brian Ellison	6	2	33%
Henry Daly	6	2	33%
Phil Middleton	6	2	33%
Sue Gardner	6	2	33%
Tim Vaughan	22	7	32%

Trainer	Runners	Wins	Strike rate (%)
Dr Richard Newland	19	6	32%
David Pipe	31	9	29%
Gary Moore	14	4	29%
Paul Nicholls	7	2	29%
Stuart Coltherd	7	2	29%
Dianne Sayer	15	4	27%
Gordon Elliott	12	3	25%
Nigel Hawke	12	3	25%
Nicky Henderson	8	2	25%
Richard Woollacott	8	2	25%
Warren Greatrex	8	2	25%
Kim Bailey	9	2	22%
Peter Bowen	16	3	19%
Nigel Twiston-Davies	22	4	18%
John Joseph Hanlon	11	2	18%
Alexandra Dunn	6	1	17%
Charlie Mann	6	1	17%
Paul Henderson	13	2	15%

Trainer	Runners	Wins	Strike rate (%)
Anthony Middleton	7	1	14%
Brendan Powell	7	1	14%
Sophie Leech	7	1	14%
Caroline Bailey	8	1	13%
Lucinda Russell	8	1	13%
Tom George	8	1	13%
Fergal OBrien	9	1	11%
Caroline Keevil	6	0	0%

Looking at the above Table, given that the average strike rate for all penalty carriers is around 29 per cent, we can draw a line from Dr Richard Newland (strike rate 32 per cent) downwards and exclude all trainers that had a strike rate below the average. We can then concentrate on those trainers that had a strike rate above average.

On this short-list the stand out trainers are probably the top four as they account for a fair number of penalty carriers among them. In particular Jonjo O'Neill looks to specialise in winning with horses carrying a penalty and he is getting a strike rate of 44 per cent off of 34 runners running under a penalty. David Bridgewater and Dan Skelton also look to be masters in this area and David Bridgewater had a strike rate of 73 per cent and Dan Skelton had a strike rate of 50% over the study period.

The next question is whether, if you just follow the trainers with the best record with penalty carriers, would you make a profit at level stakes? The simple answer is yes. Simply following this group of trainers would result in a strike rate of around 39 per cent, which is even better than following penalty carriers blindly. If you just backed their penalty carriers at the Betfair Starting Price then, according to my database over four years, you would make a return of about 15 pence for every pound invested. That isn't a bad return on investment. The number of selections isn't huge but you should make about 100 bets per year under this system.

Can the Dosage Index give punters an edge?

To readers of these pages this will be obvious to all, but to be a profitable punter you need new angles, especially ones that aren't picked up by others. One area that I think gets overlooked in National Hunt racing in an analysis of the horses pedigree. In contrast, there are plenty of people that look at the pedigree of a horse in flat racing, such as trying to work out from a horses sire and grandsire whether or not it is likely to stay the distance of the Derby or St Leger. However, in National Hunt racing pedigree rarely gets discussed because most punters and people in the racing media think that all that needs to be known about a horse is in the form book. After all horses in National Hunt racing can race over many seasons, under all kinds of conditions. This though is a false assumption and chasers and hurdlers are often attempting new distances or racing over different types of going that may or may not be suit them.

I first became interested in trying to use pedigree analysis in National Hunt racing when I read an excellent book called 'Narrowing the

Field: Using The Dosage Method to Win at National Hunt Racing' by Ben Aiken. This got be interested became the author had done some painstaking research on all the big jump races and had looked at the statistical trends to see whether certain races were suited to horses with particular pedigrees or, to be more precise, whether the race winners had a certain type of Dosage profile.

For those not familiar with Dosage I'll give a quick summary. Basically, the Dosage Index is a simple statistical formula to work out whether a horse is basically bred for speed or stamina by an analysis of the horse's pedigree. It was first developed in the early 20th century, when a French researcher, Lt. Col. J. J. Vullier, looked at whether certain sires were more likely to pass on speed or stamina to their offspring. However, it t wasn't until until 1981 Kentucky Derby that dosage became more widely known. In that year the Daily Racing Form – the equivalent of the Racing Post in the United States - published Dosage figures for that years race that were based on a new version of the system produced by an American scientist called Dr. Steve Roman. The Dosage Index successfully predicted which horses would stay of the mile-and-a-quarter distance of the Kentucky Derby.

The Dosage index is based on a list of key sires in the first four generations of a horse's pedigree. These key, or chef-de-race sires, are grouped into one or two of the following categories: Brilliant, Intermediate, Classic, Solid or Professional, with "Brilliant" indicating that the sire's progeny fared best at very short distances and "Professional" denoting a strong stamina influence. The other three categories sit in between on a continuum. The list is updated and is based on an evidenced based assessment of a sires speed or stamina influence.

In terms of calculating the Dosage profile, if a horse's sire is on the chef-de-race list, it counts 16 points for the group to which the sire belongs (or eight in each of two categories if the sire was placed in two groups); a grandsire counts eight points, a great-grandsire four, and a great-great-grandsire gets two points.

To give an example Pleasant Company just failed to win the 2018 Grand National over an extended four miles. He was 25-1 but his pedigree was heavy on stamina because he had no 'brilliant' (i.e. speed sires in his pedigree and so had no 'brilliant' points in his pedigree. He had just one point in the 'intermediate' and 'classic' categories of his pedigree but had four points in the 'solid' and four points in the 'professional' categories of his pedigree, which are the categories that reflect stamina.

In terms of the Dosage Index (DI) this means that Pleasant Company had a DI of 0.18. This is the ratio in points between speed and stamina. The calculation is done by adding his points in the brilliant and intermediate categories together and then adding half of his 'classic' points to that total. This gives Pleasant Company 1.5 points in the speed half of his pedigree.

On the stamina side of his pedigree he has 0.5 points from his 'classic' score combined with the four points from his 'solid' and four points from his 'professional' scores. This gives him 8.5 stamina points. The dosage index is then his speed points (1.5) divided by his stamina points (8.5). This gives an index of 0.18, which is well under one and indicates a pedigree strong on stamina. Had you done for the same calculation for the winner Tiger Roll you would have come up with a Dosage Index of 0.58, which indicates a strong stamina influence but not to the same extent as Pleasant Company. This was perhaps reflected in the finish with Pleasant Company staying on very strongly and just failing to reel in Tiger Roll. Fortunately the excellent website www.pedigreequery.com does all the hard work for you and gives you the Dosage Profiles of every horse on its database.

If Dosage is to mean anything in National Hunt racing I figured that the place to start would be the Grand National because it is a race over such an extreme distance and is run at a strong pace. It therefore requires a high degree of stamina. As you can see from Table 1, the winners of the race generally have a low DI (i.e. below one), with 14 out of the last 21 winners of the race having a DI under 1.

Dosage Profile of Grand National Winners 1998 to 2018

Year	Winner	B	I	C	S	P	DI
2018	Tiger Roll	2	0	15	9	0	0.58
2017	One For Arthur	4	0	9	4	1	0.89
2016	Rule The World	4	2	3	7	4	0.6
2015	Many Clouds	2	1	15	4	0	0.91
2014	Pineau De Re	0	0	1	1	0	0.33
2013	Auroras Encore	5	0	10	5	4	0.71
2012	Neptune Collonges	0	0	0	2	0	0
2011	Ballabriggs	1	1	2	4	2	0.43
2010	Don't Push It	6	5	12	4	1	1.55

Year	Winner	B	I	C	S	P	DI
2009	Mon Mome	1	1	2	0	0	3
2008	Comply or Die	2	0	6	4	0	0.71
2007	Silver Birch	2	0	4	8	6	0.25
2006	Numbersixvalverde	2	0	0	6	2	0.25
2005	Hedgehunter	8	3	8	2	7	1.15
2004	Amberleigh House	5	1	8	2	4	1
2003	Monty's Pass	3	4	6	0	7	1
2002	Bindaree	1	1	3	4	1	0.54
2001	Red Marauder	0	5	0	1	0	5
2000	Papillon	0	1	4	1	6	0.33
1999	Bobbyjo	5	1	4	6	4	0.67
1998	Earth Summit	3	0	11	2	0	1.13

This though means that 1/3rd of the winners have had speed biased pedigrees. For example, Mon Mome, Red Marauder, Earth Summit, Hedgehunter, and Don't Push It all had a surprising degree of speed in their pedigrees. Clearly the Dosage Index isn't a perfect winning formula for predicting stamina in a horses pedigree. This though doesn't mean to say it can't give you an edge.

However, looking at just the winners of races can be misleading. You really need to compare the winners to the losers to work out if Dosage can differentiate between the two. This is hard to do without a database of dosage ratings and racing results, which isn't available. Instead I continued with the Grand National and looked at the 2018 renewal to see if Dosage could discriminate in some way.

Runners for the 2018 Grand National and Dosage Profiles

Name	Age	Weight	Odds	B	I	C	S	P	DI
Tiger Roll (IRE)	8	10-13	10/1	2	0	15	9	0	0.58
Pleasant Company (IRE)	10	10-11	25/1	0	1	1	4	4	0.18
Bless The Wings (IRE)	13	10-06	40/1	3	2	10	9	2	0.63
Anibale Fly (FR)	8	11-08	10/1	1	2	9	3	5	0.6
Milansbar (IRE)	11	10-06	25/1	2	0	8	4	6	0.43
Road To Riches (IRE)	11	10-05	40/1	1	0	7	2	4	0.47
Gas Line Boy (IRE)	12	10-11	25/1	3	0	13	2	2	0.9
Valseur Lido (FR)	9	11-07	66/1	2	1	3	0	0	3
Vieux Lion Rouge (FR)	9	10-13	25/1	0	0	0	2	0	0

Name	Age	Weight	Odds	B	I	C	S	P	DI
Raz De Maree (FR)	13	10-09	20/1	0	0	5	5	2	0.26
Baie Des Iles (FR)	7	10-08	16/1	4	1	5	2	2	1.15
Blaklion	9	11-10	14/1	3	0	15	4	0	0.91
The Last Samuri (IRE)	10	11-08	20/1	4	2	7	3	2	1.12
Total Recall (IRE)	9	11-05	7/1	2	2	11	2	1	1.12
Alpha Des Obeaux (FR)	8	11-04	33/1	3	1	6	4	0	1
Perfect Candidate (IRE)	11	11-03	40/1	1	0	12	7	2	0.47
Shantou Flyer (IRE)	8	11-02	25/1	3	2	13	3	1	1.1
Tenor Nivernais (FR)	11	11-01	66/1	0	0	5	1	2	0.45
Carlingford Lough (IRE)	12	11-01	33/1	4	0	6	4	0	1
Chase The Spud	10	10-12	25/1	2	1	8	4	5	0.54
Warriors Tale	9	10-12	28/1	5	0	6	2	1	1.33
Seeyouatmidnight	10	10-12	11/1	3	0	6	3	0	1
The Dutchman (IRE)	8	10-11	25/1	4	1	7	4	0	1.13
Ucello Conti (FR)	10	10-10	16/1	1	0	6	3	0	0.67
Saint Are (FR)	12	10-10	50/1	0	0	6	8	2	0.23

Name	Age	Weight	Odds	B	I	C	S	P	DI
I Just Know (IRE)	8	10-08	16/1	0	0	5	1	0	0.71
Virgilio (FR)	9	10-08	66/1	1	0	1	2	0	0.6
Maggio (FR)	13	10-08	66/1	5	1	7	1	0	2.11
Pendra (IRE)	10	10-08	40/1	2	0	10	4	0	0.78
Buywise (IRE)	11	10-08	40/1	2	2	10	2	0	1.29
Childrens List (IRE)	8	10-08	40/1	0	1	3	4	2	0.33
Lord Windermere (IRE)	12	10-07	50/1	2	0	6	8	2	0.38
Captain Redbeard (IRE)	9	10-07	20/1	3	2	8	7	0	0.82
Houblon Des Obeaux (FR)	11	10-07	33/1	2	0	13	5	0	0.74
Final Nudge (IRE)	9	10-06	33/1	2	0	10	4	0	0.78
Double Ross (IRE)	12	10-06	40/1	0	0	0	4	12	0
Thunder and Roses	10	10-05	33/1	0	1	1	4	2	0.23
Delusionsofgrandeur (IRE)	8	10-05	50/1	3	1	12	10	0	0.63

The average DI of the 38 runners is indeed below 1 (0.78) and 26 of the field have a DI below one (68 per cent). Of the 12 horses to finish the race, nine had a DI below one and that also means that nine out of the

26 runners (35 per cent) with a DI below one finished the race. In contrast just three of the 12 runners with a DI above one finished the race (25 per cent).

The Figure below also suggests that there is a relationship between the Dosage Index and horses finishing position in the Grand National.

Relationship between Dosage Index (DI) ranked lowest (rank 1) to highest (rank 38) and finishing positions

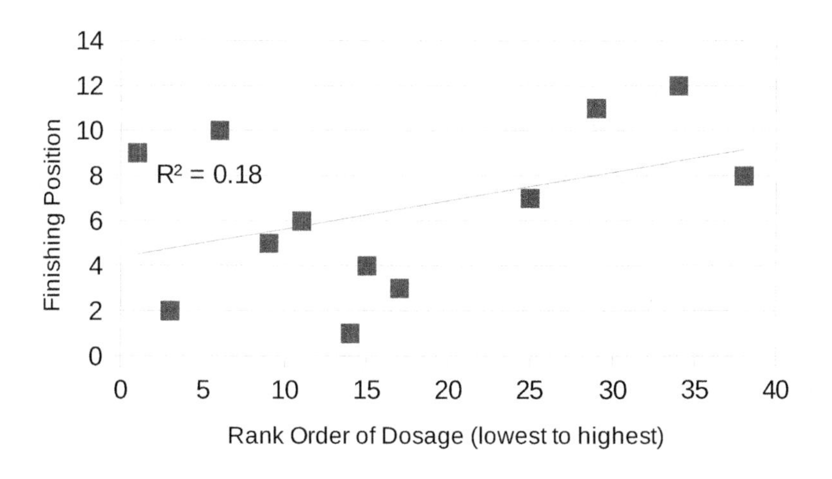

The data therefore suggests that horses ranked lowest in terms of their DI scores also had lower finishing positions. The relationship is not massively strong but there is nevertheless some evidence to suggest that you are better off betting horses with a low DI in the Grand National. I'd certainly be sceptical of horses that hadn't proven their stamina and didn't have a DI to suggest that they might stay the trip.

What can we conclude from this analysis about the Dosage Index as a betting system? Using the example of the Grand National there would appear to be some merit in using the Dosage Index to work out whether or not a horse has the necessary stamina for long distance races over the jumps. This does not mean that a horse can't win a staying chase with a high Dosage Index but overall there would appear to be some advantage to siding with horses with plenty of stamina in their four generation pedigree. As this information is not readily available to other punters you might be able to use this information to your advantage but you would need to build it into a system with other selection factors to narrow down the number of selections per race.

The handicap débutante system

The first thing to say about the handicap débutante system is that it isn't a desperately complicated system. However, it does have a solid rationale as it is about backing unexposed runners in handicaps.

The idea of a handicap is that the official handicapper assesses the form of all the runners in a race and then allots them weights with the aim of equalising the chances of every runner. This isn't an exact science by any means but generally speaking handicap races are often ultra-competitive and the official handicapper of the British Horse racing Authority (BHA) does a fairly good job.

Handicap races are loved by bookmakers as they help to ensure large field sizes. This is because owners and trainers will want their horses to compete in handicap races because even if their horse isn't a world beater it will be given a weight, which in theory at least, should give it a squeak in every handicap that it contests. Bookmakers therefore love handicap because they are competitive and feature lots of runners. This is good for turnover and guarantees lots of losing punters, which in turn means big profits for bookmakers. It therefore isn't surprising that bookmakers spend a lot of money sponsoring handicap races.

Handicap races though do give the astute punter a chance because a handicap is only as competitive as the official handicapper's judgement. If the official handicapper gets it wrong then they can end up underestimating a horse's chance and allocating it a low weight. This can happen for a variety of different reasons. Some trainers are very adept as helping to disguise the true ability of their animals so that when they run in a handicap for the first time the poor official handicapper really hasn't got a clue as to how good the horse may be. This can mean that a horses chance is seriously underestimated and the horse can end up with a BHA handicap mark that is well below what it should have received had its true ability been known.

I know of at least one trainer that is expert at discovering the true ability of his horses in gallops at home. He then runs them over an inadequate distance or over unsuitable going in non-handicap races until they have had at least three races to be qualified for a handicap race. Once qualified for a handicap they are then ready to run over the right distance and going. The official handicapper though knows nothing of this. He or she only has the form book to rely upon and they simply see a horse that has been well-beaten in three previous races. They therefore get a lowly handicap rating that is well below what it should have been. No rules of racing have been broken here. It is simply a shrewd trainer doing his best for his owners and helping those in the know to win a few quid. However, you don't need to be one of those in the know to profit from these runners, provided that one is patient and prepared to follow a simple system over a large number of races.

My simple system is to back three-year –olds when they are making their handicap début in an all-age handicap. Following this simple system from 2005 onwards would have netted you a 20 per cent return on all stakes invested. This was based on betting the selection at the Betfair SP, and taking off a 5 per cent commission rate on all winning bets. This was over a sample of nearly 2,000 selections over the last few years. Unfortunately the strike rate was low at below 10 per cent. Therefore one needs to be patient because when the system gets it right the odds of reward on winning selections are high. The average winning Betfair Starting Price in my sample was nearly 18-1!

The rationale for focusing on three-year-olds in all-age handicaps is that three-year-old handicap débutantes are particularly unexposed in comparison to their older rivals. The handicapper is particularly unsighted on these types of animals because three-years obviously don't have as much form in the book as a four or five year old handicapper that has been contesting handicaps for some time. The handicapper has a good grip on these animals and will know them inside out. They are likely to be weighted right up to their ability. In contrast the three year is normally still maturing across the season and may still be improving. In some rare cases the three-year old may be making a début in a handicap because they haven't quite matured in time to compete in the top class conditions races. For instance, some of the big trainers like Sir Michael Stoute have horses that are bred to win classics but don't reach their potential in time. They are then given opportunities later in the season to contest valuable handicaps.

These animals can sometimes progress from handicaps to Group races towards the back end of the season.

In summary, backing three year old handicap débutantes in all-age handicaps can be profitable if you are prepared to tolerate a low strike rate. The system seems to do well over a large sample and has a good underlying rationale.

The Jump-to-profit system

I want to share with you a simple system that I developed for the 'winter game' a few years ago called Jump-to-profit. It is a system that has demonstrated consistent results over a number of years. I'm not claiming that it is going to make anyone rich but in sharing the system with you I hope that I can offer you a few ideas that you can incorporate into your own research, and offer a few pointers about how to develop your own betting systems.

Basically the Jump-to-profit system has four variables. These are based around a racehorse's class and consistency

In order to qualify as a selection a horse must fulfil the following criteria:

1) They should have been genuinely placed in each of their last three races run in Great Britain and Ireland, run under National Hunt rules.

2) In their last race they should have recorded a previous starting price ratio of 0.5 or less.

3) The class rating of the current race should NOT be more than double the value recorded in the horse's previous race.

4) The class ratings recorded by the horse in each of its last three races should be added together to produce an aggregate class rating. The selection should have the highest aggregate class rating recorded of all the runners in the race.

The above criteria will not mean much to you without a definition of some of the key terms, so below I have tried to explain what I mean by genuine placings, class ratings and the previous starting price ratio. I'll explain these rules in detail so that you can have a go at implementing the system yourself.

Genuine placings

A genuine placing is defined as a placing that bookmakers would recognise in each-way betting.

In each-way betting a place is defined as:

1. A first place only if the race had fewer than 5 runners
2. Finished first or second in a race with 5, 6 or 7 runners
3. Finished first, second or third in a race of 8 runners or more
4. Finished first, second, third or fourth in a race that had 16 runners or more and was a handicap.

Defining a placing in this way is useful because you don't penalise horses that finished fourth against a huge number of runners and don't reward horses that finished second in a three horse race. This is pretty basic stuff but I know of many systems, including commercial ones, that don't make this distinction.

Previous Starting Price Ratio

You may find this surprising but the Starting Price recorded by a horse in its previous race is a strong predictor of its chance next time out. For instance, if a horse was a well backed but a beaten favourite last time it is more likely to win next time. Conversely a horse that started at odds of 40 to 1 last time has only a slim chance of winning next time. This is because the betting market contains so much information about the ability of horse and you need to make use of this information. However, you need to be aware of a bias in the previous SP. You need to take account of the number of runners in the horse's last race. For example, an even money shot that beat one other runner wasn't as well supported in the market as an even money shot that beat 10 other runners. This is why you need to calculate the previous starting price ratio.

In order to calculate this statistic you need to note the Starting Price recorded by the horse in its last race, and the number of runners from that race. This information can be found in the detailed form summaries provided by the Racing Post newspaper or website.

A horse must record a Previous Starting Price ratio of 0.5 or less to qualify under this system rule. The previous price ratio is computed by converting the horse's previous starting price to decimal odds, and dividing this figure by the number of runners recorded in the horse's last race.

The decimal odds can be computed easily with a pocket calculator by dividing the SP numerator by the denominator on a pocket calculator. For instance 5 to 1 is 5 divided by 1= 5, while 9 to 2 is 9 divided by 2=4.5 and 4 to 5 is 4 divided by 5=0.8.

Once you have converted the bookmakers odds into a decimal you should then divide the decimal odds recorded by the horse in its last race by the number of runners in that race. For example, if a horse was returned at 5 to 1 in its last race and the total number of runners in that race was 10 then the price ratio is 0.5 (5 divided by 10= 0.5).

Calculating class ratings

This is done by first considering the race penalty value for each of the horse's last three races.

The penalty value is basically the monetary value of the prize awarded to the winner of the race. It is termed the penalty value because under the rules of racing winners of races of a certain race value may earn handicap penalties the next time they run. The penalty value or 'prize' is clearly indicated in the detailed form summaries provided by Racing Post for each runner in a race, and on their web site.

Each penalty value should be divided by 1,000, and then rounded to the nearest whole number to produce a class rating for each of the horse's three previous races. In other words the class rating is calculated as 1-point for each £1,000 of race value. For example if a horse last ran in a race that was valued at £10,600 to the winner then the class rating becomes

10.6 points (£10,600 divided by £1,000=10.6). Older readers may remember the legendary system backer C Van Der Wheil of Market Harborough, who wrote a series of articles for Raceform in the 1980s. He calculated 'class' in exactly this way.

For simplicity the class rating should be rounded to the nearest integer or whole number and so the final class rating in the above example wouldn't be 10.6 but rounded to 11 points. Conversely if the value of the race was £10,450 then, after rounding to the nearest whole number, the class rating would be 10 (£10,450/£1,000=10.4). In the event that the race was valued at £10,500 (£10,500/£1,000=10.5) then you ALWAYS round up to the nearest whole number and so the class rating is 11.

The selection should be the horse that has the highest aggregate class rating in the race under study. Therefore a horse that last ran in a race valued at £10,600 (class rating=11), and previously in a race of £7,450 (class rating=7) and before that ran in a race valued at £3,500 (class rating=4) will have an aggregate class rating of 22 (11+7+4). This should be *more than or equal to the rating achieved by the next highest rated horse or horses in the race.* Thus in a four runner race if Horses A, B and C all have an aggregate class rating of 10, and Horse D has a class value of 9, then Horses A, B and C are all joint top-rated.

You will frequently calculate class ratings for horses in the same race were one runner has had three previous races and some of the other runners have only had one or two previous races. These runners will obviously tend to total a lower number of class points than those that have had three previous races. This is a bias against less experienced runners and this is intentional. It is a fact that more experienced horses have a significant edge over their less experienced rivals, independent of all other factors.

You need to monitor non-runners because a non-runner may mean that another horse in the race qualifies as a selection. This would occur, for instance, if Horse A met all the system criteria apart from the class criteria, and was rated second best on class to a non-runner. The fact that the class horse in the race is now a non-runner means that Horse A would now qualify as a selection because he now meets all the systems criteria.

Class rating change between current and last race

The class rating of the current race should be less than double the class rating of the horse's previous race. For example, if a horse was running in a race valued at £3,000 then the class rating of this race is 3. However, if the horse had previously competed in a race valued at £1,600 then the class racing for this race would be 2. The horse is therefore now stepping up in class from a class 2 race to a class 3 race. The increase between the current and previous race is 1 point. This is half the value of the horses previous race (1 divided by 2=0.5) and so the horse is running a race that was double the class rating of the horse's previous race and so the horse does NOT qualify as a selection. The situation would have been the same had the horse gone from a class 2 race to a class 5 race. The class of the current race is more than double that of the previous race. This guards us against selecting horses that might be outclassed.

After reading all of this (thank you for your patience!) you now have the bones of the system. Historically it has recorded a strike rate of around 40%. Given the nature of the system and its focus on strong form horses the selection tends to be the favourite or second favourite. Overall the average SP of selections is around 6 to 4 and so you need to ensure that you get on at the best possible odds. If you can consistently beat the SP on selections then you will greatly increase the systems rate of return. In the early years of the system this was easy because you simply bet on the exchanges as these offered better value than bookmakers SP, but with the SP market now more closely aligned with the exchange odds this is now more difficult.

A simple system for two-year old races

Not everyone will agree but I've come to love juvenile races because I have uncovered a profitable little system for them which has shown a smallish but consistent rate of return over a number of years.

When developing betting systems it often pays to keep things simple. I have found time after time that you are better off basing systems around the core form factors and then thinking about ways in which you can exploit blind spots in the market to attain value.

A few years ago I developed a simple system for two-year-old races that is based on just five simple factors. I'll first describe the system, its rationale and then go on to discuss its results.

The rules of the system are as follows:

- Select stakes races for juveniles. You need to ignore handicap races for two-year-olds. These so-called nursery events are an absolute graveyard for punters. I know some professionals believe that they can gain an edge in these events but I have often found their results to be mysterious, unless you follow certain stables that specifically target these types of event. Overall the favourite wins more often in juvenile stakes races.

- Select the clear favourite in the betting market for the non-stakes race. This doesn't mean the forecast favourite. The system assumes that in two-year-old races the betting market is the best guide and that all inside information and all relevant form are contained in the betting odds. Thus if a horse shortens significantly to be the market leader at the off then this is because those in the know have lumped on. Provided that you time your bet to the last minute before the off you can pretty much guarantee that you will have backed the favourite. This is a practical draw back for followers of the system because you need to be following the action prior to the off.

- The selection should be ridden by a non-claiming jockey or a 3lb claimer only. It doesn't happen very often but on occasion the favourite can be ridden by an inexperienced jockey, claiming an allowance of more than three pounds. Now let me ask you a question. If you combine an inexperienced two-year-old and an inexperienced jockey do you think that this is a good combination? Unless the seven-pound claimer is the next Lester Pigott I don't think that this is a good combo in which to invest. There is a greater probability that things can go wrong when you put a novice jockey on an inexperienced and highly-strung racehorse. The results of the system are much better if the favourite has the assistance of a professional or an experienced claimer that has ridden plenty of winners (i.e. three-pound claimers).

- The selection should be a colt. This may seem a bit of an odd criteria for a system but I can tell you that I have analysed thousands of races from different angles and I have consistently found that fillies and mares are more inconsistent than colts. All others things being equal you are better off backing a colt than a filly. I once put this theory to the test and conducted a detailed statistical study that basically matched the form characteristics of colts and fillies. You would have expected that both sex groups, given that they were matched on a number of form factors, would have the same win strike rate. However the fillies had a lower strike rate and this I think can only be explained by their inherent inconsistency. I've spoken to stable staff, trainers and veterinarians and they all concur that fillies are more difficult to train and they do not take their racing as well as colts. The results of this system are significantly improved if you stick to the colts. This also means that you should stay clear of two-year-old geldings. My reasoning here is that if the value of a racehorse is basically its value as a future stallion then, if you considered a juvenile to have any potential, you wouldn't cut it's balls off in its first season would you? The statistics show that two-year-old geldings that start as favourite tend to win less often than two-year colts.

- Finished fourth last time out or worse. This final factor is the main one that gives the system its edge. You would still make a profit if you simply made selections on the basis of the first four factors but by adding this fifth factor you can increase the rate of return. Why though would you want to back horses that finished outside of the first three on their last start? Good question and most punters probably wouldn't want to back a horse that had this profile. And this is exactly why we gain an edge by adding this factor. If plenty of fellow punters don't like horses that finished fourth or unplaced last time out but the horse still went off favourite this tells us that the horse must have plenty else in its favour and it probably has its connections backing it. Basically the odds on offer are greater than the true probability of the horse winning. This is the definition of value. In going against the crowd we gain an edge. Furthermore finishing unplaced last time out in a two-year-old race isn't the negative that it would be in other types of race. Juvenile races often have big fields and so finishing fifth in a 15-runner race is a better effort than finishing third in an eight-runner race. Punters though often ignore field sizes when evaluating form. Juveniles also often run below form on their first few starts as they start to learn their trade. Finishing unplaced on their early starts is therefore not necessarily a negative. It is potential that counts and if a horse still gets market support, despite a poor placing in the recent past, then it is expected to improve.

A number of so-called profitable systems do not record consistent levels of profit, year in, and year out. They often record a lucky year in which they make an extraordinary profit, which disguises the fact that in a normal year the system makes a loss. When testing systems it is therefore important to look to see if a system makes a profit over a number of different years. I am always much more confident of a system that has shown a consistent profit over time.

My results, taken over a three-year period, show that the simple system outlined found 366 selections and had 165 winners, representing a strike rate of over 45 per cent. This keeps losing runs short and is good from a psychological point of view because you are frequently at the payout window. The overall profit to a 1-point stake was almost £56, giving a rate of return of over 15 per cent. A profit was recorded in all years.

Further analysis shows that selections that were beaten favourites last time out, had under four starts, and ran on turf rather than the all-weather had a higher rate of return. This information could be developed into a staking plan to ensure that maximum stakes went on selections that historically had earned the highest rate of return.

Profiting from form figure combinations

There are a great number of betting systems on horse racing that are based around a horse's previous finishing positions. I recall that one of the first systems that I ever read was based around such a method.

The system cost me twenty-five quid and it involved awarding points according to where the horse had finished in its last two races. As you would expect the maximum number of points were awarded to the horse that had finished first in its last two starts. A horse could only score points if it had finished in the first four. No other form factors were considered

The simplicity of the system caused me concern. For instance, it didn't take into account whether the horse had finished first in a two horse race or had been placed fifth in a thirty runner handicap. Furthermore, it didn't consider the class of the horse's previous races, and so you could in theory award a maximum number of points to a horse that had won two sellers at Southwell on its last two starts and was now running at Royal Ascot.

The system also didn't consider the distance of the race, and whether the horse was now racing over a distance radically different from what it had done before. It also didn't take account of the horse's jockey or trainer, and it paid no consideration to the going, or the number of days since the horse previously raced. I therefore concluded that the system was far too simplistic to be worth following, and decided to cut my losses. I was already twenty-five pounds down and didn't fancy losing any more.

However, more recently I revisited my original form figure system and tested it to see how it performed over a large sample of previous races. I was surprised to find that the method did produce reasonable results. You wouldn't have made a profit, but you would have done a good deal better using this system than if you had made selections at random. This led me to look again at systems based on form figure combinations. I was now curious to see whether it was possible to make a profit from such a simple approach.

The merit of recent finishing positions

The first thing that I analysed was the statistical probabilities of a horse winning according to its finishing position on it last, second from last, and third from last start for all flat races run in Great Britain in recent years. The results of these analyses are presented in Tables 1, 2 and 3.

Table 1: Finishing position on last start and % win on next start

Finishing pos.	Winners	Losers	Total	% Win
First	5,384	26,412	31,796	16.9
Second	5,428	26,072	31,500	17.2
Third	4,125	27,122	31,247	13.2
Fourth	3,265	27,191	30,456	10.7
Fifth	2,657	26,270	28,927	9.2
Sixth	2,081	24,579	26,660	7.8
Seventh	1,669	22,470	24,139	6.9

Finishing pos.	Winners	Losers	Total	% Win
Eighth	1,409	19,977	21,386	6.6
Ninth	1,081	17,248	18,329	5.9
Tenth +	3,546	70,424	73,970	4.8
Total	30,645	287,765	318,410	9.6

Table 2: Finishing position on second from last start and % win on next start

Finishing pos.	Winners	Losers	Total	% Win
First	4,141	25,602	29,743	13.9
Second	4,229	25,243	29,472	14.3
Third	3,546	25,385	28,931	12.3
Fourth	2,937	25,057	27,994	10.5
Fifth	2,440	24,000	26,440	9.2
Sixth	2,043	22,131	24,174	8.5
Seventh	1,750	19,923	21,673	8.1
Eighth	1,424	17,616	19,040	7.5
Ninth	1,120	15,208	16,328	6.9
Tenth +	3,951	60,753	64,704	6.1
Total	29,924	291,596	321,520	9.3

Table 3: Finishing position on third from last start and % win on next start

Finishing pos.	Winners	Losers	Total	% Win
First	3,434	23,938	27,372	12.5
Second	3,478	23,798	27,276	12.8
Third	3,061	23,609	26,670	11.5
Fourth	2,628	22,955	25,583	10.3
Fifth	2,220	21,836	24,056	9.2
Sixth	1,893	19,957	21,850	8.7
Seventh	1,636	17,867	19,503	8.4
Eighth	1,403	15,680	17,083	8.2
Ninth	1,121	13,442	14,563	7.7
Tenth +	4,071	53,344	57,415	7.1
Total	30,352	293,954	324,306	9.4

The data presented in Tables 1,2 and 3 reveal a number of facts that are worth discussing further.

It found it interesting that the finishing position recorded on a horse's last start is more predictive of a win next time than the horses finishing position on its second from last, and third from last start. For example, the win rate for those horses that won their last race was 16.9 per cent. But the win rate for those horses that won on their second last start was only 13.9, and the rate was a meagre 12.5 for those horses that recorded a win on their third from last start.

The system that I described earlier didn't take heed of this fact because it weighted the finishing position recorded for a horse's last and second from last start as being of equal importance.

You probably noticed from Tables 1,2 and 3 that second placing were more predictive of a win next time out than any other finishing position, including previous wins. This applies to whether the finishing position was recorded for the horses last, second or third from last run. This makes nonsense of all those systems that award the greatest number of points for winning performances. The greatest number of points should actually be awarded for second places.

It is worth speculating why second places record a higher strike rate than previous wins. The most probable explanation is that last-time-out winners find themselves running against better horses the next time they race, either because the handicapper gives them a higher rating, or because the horse's connections become more ambitious. Whatever the reason previous winners are set a greater task the next time they race. In contrast the horse that finishes second tends not to experience a significant change in its handicap rating. It can consequently compete next time against roughly similar opposition. In addition, the connections of runners-up have no good reason to raise their horse in class if it has already been beaten at a lower grade.

System development

In terms of system development one could try to use the probabilities presented in tables 1, 2 and 3 to develop a revised scoring system that awarded the maximum number of points for horses that record three previous second places. This would be logical but it does not take into account the possibility that different form figure combinations may record a higher win rate. For instance, horses that record form figures of 112 may have a higher win rate than horses that have three seconds to their name. As a result I decided to research form figure combinations for different types of races rather than develop a revised point scoring system.

In my analysis I considered only a horse's last three previous finishing positions. I did this because the predictive value of form figures declines with time. For instance, as seen in tables 1 and 3, a win last time out is more predictive of a win next time than a win that is recorded on a horse's third from last run. The number of form figure combinations also becomes too large if one starts to consider more than three previous performances. I also re-classified form figures into six categories as follows:

- First (denoted by the figure '1')
- Second ('2')
- Third ('3')
- Fourth ('4')
- Fifth or any other placing (0). This category included horses that refused to start, were pulled-up or brought down etc.
- No run (if the horse had not previously raced, or had raced only once or twice).

I categorised the data in this way because if one starts to analyse all placing the number of form figure combinations become too numerous.

The form figures were also derived on a first-past-the-post basis. In other words if a horse was disqualified and its placing changed by the stewards I ignored the revised placing and used the original finishing order (i.e. as the horses past the finishing post). I did this because I have often found that, in the event of intervention by the stewards, it is the original result that more accurately reflects the merit of each runner.

It should also be noted that I did not distinguish between form figures recorded across different racing seasons. Thus if I read in my racing paper the form figures '1-21' I ignored the seasonal delimiter (-) and interpreted the combination as 121 (the figure on the right being for the horses most recent start).

The results

In the tables that follow I present the results of my findings for different form figure combinations, for different types of races. Due to space I have only included those combinations that returned a profit, and I have only included those combinations that had a sample of at least fifty. This makes the results more reliable.

Non juvenile stakes races

Non-juvenile stakes races record a total of twenty profitable form figure combinations. Table 4 shows that backing only those horses that recorded one of these combinations would have netted a return of just over 11 per cent. Indeed some of the combinations record extraordinary profits. But don't get excited. You have to be cautious about the bigger returns because they tend to come from the smaller samples. For instance the combination 2,4,2 returns an 80 per cent profit but the sample is only 59. In contrast, the combination 1,2,0 returns just 2 per cent but on a sample of 371. This is probably the more reliable finding and one could be confident that this combination would return a profit in the future. Small returns though are not always associated with the larger samples. The form figure triple of 2,3,0 produces a rate of return of nearly 15 per cent and is based on a sample of 228 selections.

A placing on either the horses last, second from last or third from last run seems to be highly important in this type of race, with all of the 20 combinations recording at least one placing (either first, second or third). It is also interesting that 8 of the 20 profitable combinations show at least one first place. It doesn't seem to matter whether the win was on the horses last, second from last or third from last run.

Table 4: Non-juvenile stakes races (non-maiden)

Last run	**Second last run**	**Third last run**	**Wins**	**Total**	**%Win**	**Profit/ loss (£)**	**Profit /loss (%)**
2	4	2	10	59	16.9	47.50	80.51
4	1	4	13	71	18.3	23.00	32.39
2	2	4	22	77	28.6	27.38	35.56
3	3	2	19	80	23.8	3.71	4.64

Last run	Second last run	Third last run	Wins	Total	%Win	Profit/ loss (£)	Profit /loss (%)
1	4	2	19	83	22.9	18.05	21.74
2	2	3	28	85	32.9	15.90	18.70
3	3	3	16	86	18.6	3.78	4.40
3	2	3	16	88	18.2	13.85	15.74
3	2	4	25	90	27.8	45.78	50.87
2	4	1	17	93	18.3	9.09	9.77
2	3	2	20	94	21.3	9.82	10.44
2	1	4	23	102	22.5	3.30	3.23
4	2	1	23	121	19.0	27.39	22.64
1	1	3	41	165	24.8	0.76	0.46
1	0	4	45	223	20.2	9.62	4.31
2	3	0	38	228	16.7	33.74	14.80
4	1	0	43	239	18.0	14.15	5.92
3	2	0	43	279	15.4	2.40	0.86
0	3	2	50	324	15.4	14.84	4.58
1	2	0	89	373	23.9	8.78	2.35
Total			**600**	**2960**	**20.3**	**332.84**	**11.24**

Non-juvenile handicaps

This type of race records 13 winning form figure combinations. Again, as with non-juvenile stakes races, a recent placing seems to be important. The profits from this race category are a modest 4 per cent but the sample size is very large and as a result we can be pretty confident that these combinations will be repeated in the future. Some combinations, such as 222,441,112, show meagre returns and are probably not worth following. I would also say that combinations that record relatively low strike rates are also worth ignoring because long losing runs are more likely. As a rule of thumb I wouldn't want to bet a combination that had a strike rate of less than 15 per cent. This is a rule that I would apply to all types of race and not just to handicaps.

Table 5: Non-juvenile handicaps

Last run	Second last run	Third last run	Wins	Total	% Win	Profit/ loss (£)	Profit /loss (%)
3	4	2	29	182	15.9	29.25	16.07
3	2	1	55	284	19.4	42.79	15.07
4	4	3	25	192	13.0	16.60	8.65
4	3	1	36	221	16.3	10.00	4.52
3	3	4	31	207	15.0	9.29	4.49
2	2	4	46	255	18.0	7.95	3.12
2	1	2	73	396	18.4	12.02	3.03
4	3	3	27	217	12.4	6.46	2.98
4	1	0	107	803	13.3	19.50	2.43
1	4	1	41	246	16.7	4.97	2.02
1	1	2	115	520	22.1	4.08	0.79

Last run	Second last run	Third last run	Wins	Total	% Win	Profit/ loss (£)	Profit /loss (%)
4	4	1	25	205	12.2	1.25	0.61
2	2	2	52	293	17.7	1.38	0.47
Total			662	4,021	16.5	165.55	4.12

Juvenile maiden races

Juvenile maiden races produce a profit of nearly 11 per cent and the strike rate for four of the five winning combinations is more than 15 per cent. The sample size for some combinations though is a bit on the small side and I would want to see a bit more action before placing my hard earned cash on the form triples 3,4,0 and 3,3,0.

Table 6: Juvenile maiden races

Last run	Second last run	Third last run	Wins	Total	Win %	Profit/ loss (£)	Profit/ loss (%)
3	3	0	16	67	23.9	22.00	32.84
3	4	0	12	55	21.8	10.56	19.20
2	2	2	22	70	31.4	8.06	11.51
3	2	No run	32	87	36.8	7.11	8.18
0	3	0	24	189	12.7	2.50	1.32

Last run	Second last run	Third last run	Wins	Total	Win %	Profit/ loss (£)	Profit/ loss (%)
Total			**106**	**468**	**24.7**	**50.23**	**10.73**

Juvenile non-maiden races

This category records a terrific profit of just over 17 per cent, with some combinations recording very large returns. Some of the health warning mentioned above apply, such as small sample sizes for some form triples and low strike rates, but there are plenty of combinations that return good profits, on large samples, and have a high strike rate. For instance, the figures 022 and 31 are of particular interest.

Table 7: Juvenile non-maidens

Last run	Second last run	Third last run	Wins	Total	% Win	Profit/ loss (£)	Profit/ loss (%)
2	1	3	24	91	26.4	85.42	93.87
2	0	2	26	97	26.8	37.13	38.27
0	2	2	20	107	18.7	37.81	35.34
0	1	1	25	168	14.9	53.96	32.12
3	2	1	15	69	21.7	14.23	20.62

Last run	Second last run	Third last run	Wins	Total	% Win	Profit/ loss (£)	Profit/ loss (%)
4	1	No run	17	95	17.9	19.44	20.47
2	2	No run	10	52	19.2	9.79	18.83
4	0	2	11	77	14.3	13.01	16.89
2	4	0	21	98	21.4	15.60	15.92
2	2	2	18	69	26.1	9.27	13.43
2	0	4	18	92	19.6	12.25	13.32
0	2	1	16	152	10.5	17.75	11.68
3	1	No run	32	147	21.8	15.87	10.80
0	3	2	15	99	15.2	9.15	9.24
0	1	3	25	159	15.7	9.43	5.93
0	4	2	11	80	13.8	4.18	5.22
1	3	3	14	79	17.7	3.25	4.11
2	1	0	31	159	19.5	1.73	1.09
3	1	3	9	59	15.3	0.58	0.97
1	0	3	17	119	14.3	0.42	0.35
1	2	3	22	103	21.4	0.06	0.06
Total			397	2,171	18.3	370.30	17.06

Maiden races for three-year-olds and older horses

Maiden races for three year olds and older horses are an interesting race category because races of this type often comprise horses that are of classic potential and ones that are completely useless. From a form figure perspective they also provide rich pickings, showing a rate of return of nearly 18 per cent. Again be aware of the health warnings that I have already mentioned and note combinations like 002, 222, and 330. They show decent profits on a high strike rate and are based on reasonable sample sizes.

Table 8: Three-year-old plus maiden races

Last run	Second last run	Third last run	Wins	Total	% Win	Profit/ loss (£)	Profit /loss (%)
0	4	3	16	76	21.1	52.37	68.90
3	2	2	31	82	37.8	43.80	53.41
4	0	3	17	79	21.5	28.25	35.76
4	2	2	19	62	30.6	20.76	33.48
0	2	4	20	82	24.4	18.28	22.29
3	2	3	22	62	35.5	12.29	19.82
2	2	4	19	51	37.3	9.81	19.24
0	4	0	51	411	12.4	60.88	14.81
0	0	2	51	287	17.8	37.37	13.02
2	2	2	41	107	38.3	9.38	8.77
3	3	0	28	117	23.9	9.92	8.48
3	0	2	21	86	24.4	4.94	5.75
4	0	2	14	59	23.7	2.91	4.93
0	3	4	16	96	16.7	2.27	2.37

Last run	Second last run	Third last run	Wins	Total	% Win	Profit/ loss (£)	Profit /loss (%)
0	2	2	35	114	30.7	1.09	0.95
Total			401	1,771	22.6	314.3	17.75

Nursery races

I also analysed the form figure combinations for nursery races but I couldn't find any profits that were worth reporting.

Debutantes

You may wonder whether I considered the record of horses that were making there race course appearance. I did and you should know that debutantes tend to record a win rate of between seven and eight per cent and you record a huge loss by blinding backing this type of animal. A study of the betting market, and a good knowledge of a horses breeding are probably the only ways to profit from previously unraced horses.

In conclusion, the simplest way to study form is to study form figure combinations. Most serious backers and racing professionals would sneer at such an approach, and for many years I personally felt that the method was naive. However, this probably explains why certain form figure combinations show a profit! If the serious backers are paying them little notice then it opens up the prospect of obtaining a bit of value.

I would suggest that you back any one of the form figure combinations I have discussed, provided that the combination records a strike rate of at least 15 per cent. This will avoid long losing runs. You could be even more discerning than this and back only those form triples that have a strike rate of at least 20 per cent.

On occasion you will find that a number of horses qualify for a bet in the same race. The figures I have produced above assume that you would back them all. You could be more selective and introduce some other filter. A good one might be to back the one with the shortest forecast price.

The Dead Eight System

You can spend a lot of time studying the form. I know of at least one leading racing tipster who practically leads a nocturnal existence by spending all night analysing the form of the runners for the following days racing. There are no doubt countless other professional and semi-professional punters who follow the same lifestyle in order to make their racing pay. I have certainly been part of this group from time to time, but in recent years, with the arrival of two young children, sleep has become more of a priority! I have therefore looked at short cutting the selection process by developing systems that use the betting market as a guide to winners.

The betting market is a good short cut because it basically reflects the views of the thousands of punters and bookmakers who have bothered to study the form. As a general guide the betting market is not too far off the mark, and the odds on offer closely match the actual statistical probabilities of a horse making it into the winner's enclosure. However, the market can have blind spots and in this section I explain a system that I call the 'the dead-eight system'. It exploits a blind spot in the market concerning each-way bets in eight runner races.

As you probably know you can place an each-way bet in a seven-runner race and if your horse finishes third the bookmakers wouldn't pay out. The horse would need to finish first or second in a seven-runner race in order to qualify as a successful each-way bet. However, in an eight runner race the rules change and you would be paid out on a horse that finished third.

This gives you a statistical edge because you now have three chances to collect on your each way bet compared to just two in a race with between five and seven runners. In terms of the percentages this means that you have a 38 per cent chance of collecting on each way bet in an eight runner race (3 possible places / 8 runners=38 per cent) compared to just 29 per cent in a seven runner race (2 possible places / 7 runners=29 per cent). In Table 1 I have detailed the probabilities of landing a successful each-way bet in races with between 5 and 30 runners.

Table 1: Probabilities of achieving a pay-out on an each-way bet

Runners	No of EW places	% Prob of placing
5	2	40.0
6	2	33.3
7	2	28.6
8	3	37.5
9	3	33.3
10	3	30.0

Runners	No of EW places	% Prob of placing
11	3	27.3
12	3	25.0
13	3	23.1
14	3	21.4
15	3	20.0
16	4	25.0
17	4	23.5
18	4	22.2
19	4	21.1
20	4	20.0
21	4	19.0
22	4	18.2
23	4	17.4
24	4	16.7
25	4	16.0
26	4	15.4
27	4	14.8
28	4	14.3
29	4	13.8
30	4	13.3

Naturally some of the statistical biases in each-way betting are reflected in the betting odds but you can nevertheless back the second favourite each-way in an eight runner race when the favourite is odds-on and make a small profit of between 7 and 8 per cent on turnover. For instance, over the last seven seasons you would have made 505 bets on this system and landed 328 successful each-way bets (a strike rate of over 65 per cent) returning a level stakes profit of £37, or a rate of return of 7.4 per cent.

The astute of you would also have noticed that each-way betting on five runner races also has a high probability of success. I can tell you that betting the second favourite each-way in these races when the favourite is odds-on also yields a small profit of around three per cent on turnover.

However, you can increase profits by betting for a place on the betting exchanges. Betting to place makes a big difference to the results of the 'dead eight system' because you save on the losing win part of an each-way bet. This can result in a big saving because the second favourite only manages to turnover the odds-on favourite once in every five races (20 per cent), but manages to place 65 per cent of the time. Thus by betting the second favourite to place rather than each-way you can turn 7 per cent profit into one of 19 per cent. When you consider that many professional punters work to achieve a much lower rate of return then these profits look very respectable.

There are a couple of points that you need to bear in mind. Firstly you need to be taking value on your place bets on the exchanges. The liquidity in these markets is often quite low and so odds can fluctuate wildly. Basically I work out the value of a place bet by comparing the bookmakers win odds and dividing this figure by the each-way betting fraction. For example, a 5 to 1 shot is at 1/5th the odds a place, is even money to be placed. I would therefore want around this figure before bothering to bet, and might want a bit more on if the place odds exceeded this benchmark.

The other thing you need to do is to watch the betting market very closely. The dead eight system depends on backing the second favourite. This is easier said than done because you don’t know which horse is definitely going to start the race as the second favourite. You therefore have to watch the market carefully and place your bet at the last possible moment before the off to be sure that you are on the second favourite. Obviously in some races it is pretty clear which horse will be the second favourite but when you have a very long odds on favourite you need to keep a close eye on which horse will go off second best in the market. This is because the odds of the other runners can merge together. In the event of joint or co second favourites you could either give the race a miss or bet the horse that you think deserves to be the second favourite.

As well as watching out for the second favourite in the market you also need to make sure that there is an odds on favourite in the race. This needs to be watched for closely if a favourite is trading in and around odds of 10 to 11 or even money.

This simple system has been proven to exploit a blind spot in the betting market concerning each-way and place betting in eight and five runner races. If you put the time in to run it properly then it can produce a decent long-term profit.

9 NEW TOOLS OF THE TRADE

The rate of technological change this century has been staggering. Had you told me twenty years ago that I could program my central heating to come on, my oven to heat up and my stereo to play Abba's Dancing Queen when I walk through the door, and I could do all of this from my mobile phone I would have thought it was a lot of nonsense.

New technology is having all kinds of impacts on punting. One good example is in-play betting. The advent of the betting exchanges and the introduction of in-play betting has given rise to in-play trading. These players try to read a race to work out which horse is going well or is about to fade in the hope of backing or laying them at one price and backing or laying them at another. These players quickly realised that their profits could be greatly boosted if they exploited the latency between the live action and the relay of television and radio commentaries to other punters off-course. Some in-play traders set themselves up in racecourse trading rooms so that they could trade on their laptops over a high speed internet connection and exploit the fact that they were getting live pictures whereas everyone off-course was seeing the action several seconds behind the actual events. This though was limited by the number of traders who could squeeze into a box on the racecourse. However, the advent of low cost drones allowed a skilled operator to fly a drone fitted with a powerful digital camera around the racecourse and beam live pictures back to in-play traders in trading rooms.

The idea that punters would be using mobile computers, high speed internet, trading on a digitised exchange rather than with bookmakers, and using drones to buzz around racecourses (very dangerously in my view) would have been viewed as science fiction only a few years ago.

The use of drones by punters may be an extreme example of how new technology has been used to gain an edge. The most obvious change for punters has obviously been the widespread use of the internet and the amount of information that is now available to the punter in the digital age. The ability to process all the information that is now available is beyond human capabilities. The challenge facing the modern backer is to use new technology to help process and analyse the data to gain some unique insight from it, and identify the wheat from the chaff.

The challenge is that every bit of the data mountain is not of equal value. Much of it will be garbage. This is what data scientists call a signal and noise problem because the data is making a lot of noise but it is hard to find the signal within it to help us make better (and profitable) decisions. The successful modern backer knows that he or she is better off investing in tools or expert research that help to weed though all the data to find the really important information, and to weight it appropriately. This might mean acquiring new analytical or IT skills, and/or investing in services that can do this for them. There are now sophisticated form databases and analytical software that can help do this, along with other technology like the Betfair API that allows high-tech punters to actually develop programs that can automatically place bets on the exchange according to a set of system rules. The modern backer needs to exploit these new tools of the trade to gain an edge.

Form databases

The twenty-first century is the digital age and this has created new opportunities for racing form to be collected, stored and analysed in digital form in databases that can later be analysed by computer software. This simply makes research much easier and opens up a huge number of opportunities for the modern punter.

It wasn't always like this and while other teenagers might have been doing other things in their bedrooms I spent many hours pouring over yellowing back copies of the Racing Post and carefully recording the results of races in a ledger against which I'd develop and test new system ideas. When computers became more readily available in the late 1980s, and better PCs arrived in the 1990s, I gradually moved my paper records into a computerised database. However, this work was all done manually and I was lucky not to gain a repetitive strain injury from all the key punching.

In and around this period the first computerised form databases started to appear and I was an eager purchaser of these first offerings. Proform and Dataform offered affordable and updated form databases, and when the internet became more mainstream these databases started to offer overnight declarations and automatic daily updates. The need for manual data entry was a thing of the past and I could research and develop systems in a fraction of the time that I had in the past. It was also a financially rewarding hobby, even after expenses.

The form databases all worked in a similar way. They collated basic racecard and result data and then the software developers would create a number of innovative derived variables from the raw information to tell you things like the number of future winners from a race, whether a horse was wearing a tongue-tie for the first time and the strike rate of the horses trainer when wearing that type of equipment. These form databases are still going today and provide a huge amount of information in a user-friendly way. They also allow the user to download data from the databases into CSV or txt format that allows you to download the data into your own database or into statistical software that allows you to do more complex analysis on the data, such as fitting statistical models to the results.

The form database that I'm more familiar with is Raceform Interactive. I'm not suggesting that this is better than any other of the market alternatives but it is the one I like using, probably because I was brought up with the Raceform and Racing Post newspapers and the variables it includes are more familiar to me.

For those that do not know the software Raceform Interactive is a horse racing analysis tool, which contains the official race results plus data from Raceform's own database. It therefore claims to be the most comprehensive and authoritative database of racing form, and provided that you have a monthly subscription, you can update the database and form quickly online every day, with results, declarations and all entries. You are also able upload statistics on trainers, jockeys and pedigrees.

You are also able to store and search your own ratings; make lists of significant horses, trainers and jockeys. These can all be saved back onto the database. This feature is probably for the real form students and paddock watchers. The software also has a useful search facility that allows you to search for a horse by its name or Raceform Number. In terms of variables in the database you get all the usual stuff but also the Raceform Performance Rating (RPR) – basically the same collateral form rating as in the Racing Post – along with Raceform Split Second speed ratings.

It is also possible to download information similar to that provided by the 'Signposts' feature in the Racing Post. I've always found this a very useful edition to the newspaper and it is a good source of winner finding material. Raceform Interactive includes all the same information as in the Racing Post and therefore you can identify the hot and cold trainers, the top course trainers, trainer and jockey combinations, and horses wearing blinkers for the first time. It is also possible to call up information on horses wearing a tongue-tie and information about which horses have travelled furthest to fulfil their engagements today (and the distance travelled) and whether the jockey has only one ride at a days meeting. There is also a draw analysis feature, which is very useful.

However, probably the best part of the software is the query database function that allows you to construct systems and test them against the data in the Raceform Interactive database. Queries can be run on historical data or on the latest declarations and entries. For example, you may have developed a profitable system based on a trainer's record with horses that win on their first run as three-year olds. You can then run the query to find out if the trainer in question has any three year old debutantes declared for the following days racing. You can therefore follow a number of systems with the minimum amount of effort. The computer also does not make mistakes and so you know when you run a system against the following days declarations that the computer will have identified all the right qualifiers for you to bet on.

All the systems (or queries) you run against the database can be saved and revisited at any time When you re-run them, they will automatically be updated to include the form which has been added to the database since the last time it was run. I'm sure that this feature will help to pay for the software if you are able to develop a number of profitable systems and follow them over a period of time.

The actual database behind the program can also be exported into a CSV or other format for importing into a spreadsheet or into another database. This is a useful feature for those who want to conduct more detailed analysis on the data and/or link it to another database.

The above describes the Raceform Interactive software but it also pretty much describes the other software on the market as they have a number similarities. The one you prefer is down to personal preference.

There is one big drawback from using commercial software. You have to recognise that if you develop profitable betting strategies from them then the same insight is probably going to be found by other subscribers to the software. The fact that the software is so easy to use, compared to developing your own database, means that it cuts down the amount of hard graft but also means that a profitable angle that you find on one day might quickly lose its edge as others discover it in the same way that you found it.

I've now moved away from commercial form database software for this reason and invested in the development of my own form database. My database builds on the official results and adds in other sources of information. I buy-in the basic results data and then add in other information that I purchase or collect myself, such as various rating services, Betfair prices, sectional times data, etc. This means that I have a fairly unique set of raw information and I can then upload this information into statistical software that allows me to do more complex analysis on the data than can be done with commercial form databases. The database itself it built from MySQL, which is a free database that uses the SQL query language. You could also build something similar in other databases, such as MS-ACCESS. It depends on what you are familiar with. Even if you start from scratch there is so much help and guidance (including code examples) online that you can quickly get something set up with a bit of time and effort. You can also write a specification for the software that you want to create and issue it online via one of the freelance computer coding project websites (e.g. rentacoder, elance etc.). You can set your own price for the work but you need to be realistic. You only get what you pay for. I've gone down this route and found it a fairly affordable way of getting started quickly with your own IT project.

Statistical software

Once you have your form database you can start to analyse it. The commercial form databases offer features to easily research your own system and employ boolean logic to help you define your own variables. These are getting more and more sophisticated but there main purpose is to make the analysis easy for the user, and the downside of this as I said before is that it means that more and more people will be able to find your winning system. I've certainly found that the shelf life of system is getting shorter and I suspect that the proliferation of system building software is partly to blame.

To do more sophisticated analysis on your data you really need to be able to import it into statistical software. These used to cost a fortune but the Open Source software movement has revolutionised statistical software and there is now some very impressive and sophisticated software packages available for free. Unfortunately you still need to invest in gaining some knowledge of statistics to be able to specify the analysis that you want and to understand the output that you produce. The key concept here is to understand statistical significance in order to test whether your winning system is genuine or the result of a few fluke winners.

A piece of software that I like is PSPP (I don't think this actually stands for anything). This is a free replacement for the proprietary program SPSS, and appears very similar to it with a few exceptions. PSPP can perform descriptive statistics, T-tests, linear regression and non-parametric tests. Its back end is designed to perform its analyses as fast as possible, regardless of the size of the input data. You can use PSPP with its graphical interface or with syntax commands. The interface allows you to create analysis very quickly and is fairly user friendly. As a result it is very easy to import your data into the software and run analysis because much of what you need to do can be found in pull down menus.

I also find it useful because all the data that you have imported can be seen in the viewer and when you create a new derived variable you can check to see if it worked by simply looking at the viewer. You can then manually save the database and export it for use in other software.

However, PSPP doesn't include that many statistical tests and will frustrate statisticians that want to fit complex models to the data. It also has a few quirks and has a number of bugs. You eventually get used to them, and as long as you save your work on a regular basis the odd crash won't bother you that much because you are getting some decent software for free.

Probably the most popular Open Source statistical software is R. Basically R is a free statistical analysis packages, with the ability to produce graphics.

The R language is widely used among statisticians and data miners for developing statistical software and data analysis. In contrast to PSPP you can basically do any statistical modelling that you want in R because there is usually a module for it. There is a graphical user interface for R called R studio that is much more user friendly than the basic R software and allows you to view your data, and is excellent for de-bugging your code. The major downside of R is that it is pretty advanced and it takes a while to use the code to get it to do anything remotely useful.

However, the major benefit of using R is that you can fit some interesting models to your data, such as conditional logistic regression (called clogit within R). This is an ideal modelling tool for horse racing data and isn't a standard feature within most of the statistical software that I have previously used. The clogit package just needs you to upload it into your R software and you can start playing with it.

Conditional logistic regression is what you want if you want to get into some serious statistical modelling on horse racing data. This is because it deals with a significant problem for other statistical models that are applied to horse racing in that it considers the relative importance of form factors between the runners *within* a race, rather than across the whole population of runners within your database of racing results.

To give you an idea about this modelling problem consider a selling hurdle with two runners. You might have a horse rated 80 on your speed figures and the next best in the field might have a rating of only 70. In another two horse race, a Grade One contest, the top rated horse on your ratings might be 160, and the next best in the race might have a rating of 159. Conditional logistic regression is able to understand that it needs to put a weight on your speed ratings, to identify the most likely winner of each race, based on the relative difference between the ratings of the horses *within* the race, rather than weight the value of your speed ratings across the population of all horses, across all races. In this example conditional logistic regression would weight having a 10 pound advantage over another horse more highly than having an advantage of only one pound, even though there is a 60 pound difference between the top rated horses in the seller and the Grade One contest.

This is all pretty obvious to us humans but some computer based statistical models (especially if they are programmed by a complete idiot) can make a real hash of weighting the importance of different form factors by not understanding it is the relative value of a factor between each horse within a race that really matters and not the absolute value of the rating (or whatever factor it may be). Those that make this mistake create models that have very biased coefficients on each form factor. In our example a wrongly specified model would give a low weight to your speed ratings in terms of picking the winner of a race, whereas the clogit model would give an accurate weighting that reflects actually how important your speed rating are in picking winners.

Automating your betting and trading strategies using the Betfair Application Programming Interface (API)

Betfair pioneered the online betting exchange at the turn of the century and it remains the world's largest player in the market. The publicly traded company has something like around one million active customers, and matches over a billion bets a year, worth tens of billions of pounds.

A key development in the history of Betfair was the free access it offered its customers to the Betfair API. This revolutionised how people use betting markets in the UK. Indeed, some people are able to earn a very decent living on the Exchange by using computerised bots to place bets by using the API. Individual punters are able to use the API to develop their own trading strategies and betting tools. Numerous software vendors have developed commercial trading applications that rely on the Exchange API, and some bookmakers use the API to support their own operations.

You can use the API to build programs to place bets on the exchange around pre-defined rules and settings. In a trading strategy or value betting model, rules are formulated with 'triggers' that will initiate both entry and exit bets into the market. For example, you could create a rule that says: "When a horses weight of money reaches more than 80%, place a back bet at the current trading price" or you might have a strategy that has a rule "Place a back bet on a horse if the price exceeds 2.00 as that would represent a value bet on that horse". The API makes all of this possible.

What skills do you need to successfully automate on Betfair? You could use an out-of-the-box product like Bet Angel or Gruss software (and many others). The upside of using these products is that you can get started straight away. However, as with any commercial product that is easy to use it often means that the edge you gain by having a good strategy can just as easily be replicated by someone else using the same software. This definitely doesn't mean that you can't make decent profits from using commercial software. The software companies are endlessly updating and improving their products to make sure their customers enjoy an edge in the market by providing more triggers or indicators to help people develop profitable strategies, and have them automated on the exchanges. However, you are more likely to keep your edge for longer if you invest in your own bespoke set up as that is less likely to be replicated by others.

Developing your own software definitely isn't easy. You could pay someone to do it for you, but you always need to know enough to be able to specify what you want as precisely as possible. I actually started from scratch on my own automated betting operation after reading a book called *Automatic Exchange Betting: Automating the Betting Process – From Strategy to Execution* by Colin Magee. Sadly this book is now out of date with regards to working code as it was based on an old version of the Betfair API, but the principles of using the Betfair API and creating your own successful automated strategies still apply, and the book provides enough technical detail to help you set up on your own. Second hand copies are still knocking around.

I'll say a bit more about this book because until Colin Magee put pen to paper those that had the skills and know how to implement automated betting strategies generally did not share their work. William Benter in Hong Kong was perhaps an exception in that he published a series of academic papers and spoke at seminars on how he had successfully implemented a computerised betting operation that was raking in millions per year for him and his investors. This openness was refreshing and I'm sure sparked interest in hundreds of people that had a dream of automating their betting. The detail though was still lacking and if you wanted to start embarking on developing automated betting systems you really needed a good introductory text book to get you started. That book simply didn't exist until the publication of *Automatic Exchange Betting*.

The book provides the perfect introductory text for those wanting to develop automated betting systems. The author explains in detail what the Betfair API is all about and how you can interact with it by using a computer programming language called Perl, and a database program called MySQL. The book explains how you can use Perl and MySQL to write programs to work with Betfair's free access API.

Each Chapter of the book takes you through the process of placing a bet on Betfair automatically. It explains how you can take a list of selections and pass these to a Perl program that will be able to schedule the placing of bets prior to the off time and then record your profits and losses.

The author also shows you how to set up a database to automatically record fluctuations in the Betfair odds of every runner in every race run in Great Britain and Ireland. This can be done every few seconds prior to the off and in-running. This in itself is a hugely valuable piece of computer code that opens up endless possibilities. For instance, you can quickly build up a huge amount of data and then start to analyse this information to identify back and lay strategies based on forecasting changes in the odds of each runner in a race.

In order to get to the stage of being able to run your own programs you need to invest time and effort. You won't just be able to pick this book up off and understand its content. You will first need to study the basics of

Perl and MySQL to do that. Fortunately there is so much code on the internet, and a range of coding forums that can be very helpful in helping you to solve coding problems. You will be surprised about how quickly you can build a piece of software. There is also a fair amount of satisfaction in solving a coding problem and watching your code complete the task you set it.

Implementing automatic betting strategies isn't easy and as well as mastering Perl to some degree you will also need to ensure that you have the right hardware and software environment to run your programs. I'd recommend the Linux based free Open Source Ubuntu operating system. This can easily be installed on your PC, or alongside your usual operating system, and it runs a range of Open Source software such as R, Perl and MySQL. This set up would allow you to download your form database in MySQl, and have R interact with it to analyse and develop systems, and then use Perl to interact between the form database and the Betfair API to place bets for you on the exchange based on the systems and strategies that you have created. The only other thing you need is a reliable internet connection because there is nothing more frustrating than missing a winner or profitable trade because your Wi-Fi decided to take a break.

To a large extent I'm a real geek and statistics and coding are leisure activities for me. This might account for my lack of friends and general unworldliness. We are all different. You might be less inclined to enjoy such activities. This though doesn't mean that you can't take advantage of some of the benefits of the technological revolution that has hit the sport of horse racing. There is plenty of commercial software available. You can also employ your own coders to implement your ideas. It is the ideas that are key, and provided that you have a good imagination to continually develop new systems and strategies you should still find an edge over the rest of the crowd. Indeed you can have all the geeky technological and coding skills in the world but if you don't have good ideas and a spark of originality then you will never succeed. Creativity can never be programmed into a computer.

10 RESEARCHING YOUR OWN BETTING SYSTEMS

Developing your own betting systems and strategies is mainly a work of the imagination. Original ideas get the profits. However, you need to be able to test your brilliant idea against the data to work out whether it was indeed a brilliant idea or not. This a lot harder than you would think and you can make a lot of costly mistakes if you get the analysis wrong. In this Chapter I therefore want to give you a few tips to help you identify genuinely winning systems.

Data samples

The first thing you need to do when developing betting systems is to get hold of as much data as possible. As discussed in the previous Chapter this is fairly easy in the modern age. There is a tonne of data on the Internet and you can purchase electronic form books that allow you to download past racing results into spreadsheet packages for further analysis. There are also menu driven software packages that allow you to develop and test systems without having to bother to learn how to program a computer. Some of this stuff isn't cheap but, as we discussed previously, data and software are the fundamental tools of the trade. I look at systems development as a business and all businesses have set-up costs. The purchase of a computer, data and software are your set up costs. Once you have developed your first profitable system you can soon recoup your investment!

I wouldn't try to skimp on paying for data. You need samples that run into tens of thousands in order to generate genuinely valid and reliable systems. A computer with plenty of memory and processing power is therefore essential. I once made the mistake of buying a cheap computer that was under powered for processing the size of database that I had put together. It took the machine an age to process and it wasn't long before the useless thing burnt out!

System ideas

Once you have your data in place you then can then start to develop some ideas for a system. Nick Mordin has written a lot about this. The most relevant is probably his '*Winning without thinking*'. The key point that he makes in this text and one that I very much agree with, is that you have to be original when developing systems. If you simply re-invent systems that have been used before then you are unlikely to make a profit because if this is a genuinely good system then the factors on which it is based will already be incorporated into the betting odds. What you should be striving for is an angle that no one has really researched before, and is probably not reflected in the betting odds. In this instance you are much more likely to be able to make a long-term profit. This doesn't necessarily mean that you need to develop very complex systems. I would always advise that you should keep it simple and focus on horse race fundamentals, namely the horse's ability, jockey, trainer, pedigree, fitness and consistency, and the betting market.

Testing your ideas

Once you have your data and you have some ideas for a system then you can start testing them against the available data. This all sounds very logical but in reality there is a certain amount of circularity in developing systems. For instance, you may have an idea but cannot find the data on which to test it, and so you can't validate the system. Your system ideas therefore need to be framed around the available data. The richer you data and the more variables it contains the more system ideas you will be able to test. This is where commercial software can be limiting because they normally only allow you to manipulate a number of pre-defined variables. This makes the software easier to use as you do not need to create your own derived variables from the raw data but can restrict what you can do. That said some software products are getting more and more sophisticated and allow the user to do more and more with the underlying data in the form book.

Once you have an idea and the data to test it you can then work out whether it is profitable or not. In the test phase you may find that your system isn't profitable and so you may want to do further research on the systems variables to find the best combination, or add other variables to improve the results, and then to test it again. However, one of the early mistakes that I made, when developing a system in this way, was to develop a system on past results and then to implement it straight away.

The system I had developed looked great on the basis of past results. I was so excited by its *past* performance that I implemented it immediately, and looked forward to buying that new car, and treating the family to nice holiday. Unfortunately the system didn't work so well when I played it for real stakes. This left me perplexed. Why didn't the system work in real time? After a lot of reflection I realised that what I had actually done was to *back fit* a system to past results.

In a back fitted system selection rules are manipulated to account for a sample of previous results. For instance if the system developer finds that his or her system picks a loser, the rules are then changed slightly to eliminate this selection. Similarly some rules are changed to accommodate a long-priced winner. This process is repeated until the system produces a respectable number of winners and a decent level of profitability on past results. This is what I did when I developed my early systems. I was using the same sample of data to build my system and to refine my ideas, and using that same data to test its validity. What I should have done was use what is called a *split-half sample*.

A split half sample is exactly what it says on the tin. It is a sample that has been split into two halves. In one half of the data you develop your system. You can then play around with the variables to your hearts content until you have something that looks to be sensible and profitable. At this stage the system is a pure back fitted system. In order to test it properly you then run the system against the 'unseen' data in the other half of the sample. This is what is called the validation sample. If the system shows a profit over both samples, and provided that the samples are large enough, then you can be fairly confident that you have found a genuinely profitable system that will work when you play it for real.

When looking at commercially available systems the sign of a back fitted system is a long list of complicated selection criteria, which often appear illogical. They tend not to work when applied in real time because they are not based on sensible, proven form factors.

Racing logic

This brings me to my next point about betting systems. Regardless of any other consideration, they must conform to racing logic. It is vital that the variables used in a system are sensible. I once stood in a betting shop in open-mouthed amazement when a fellow punter punched the air to celebrate a winner and turned to me and said “First letter ‘R’ system. Never fails”. I think most right thinking people would agree that horses with a name beginning with the letter ‘R’ are no more likely to win than a horse with a name beginning with any other letter of the alphabet. There is no logic to the system. It is better to stick to variables that most racing professionals would agree are important to winner findings. You can then combine these variables in unique ways.

If you are really imaginative you might be able to develop a variable that measures a form concept in an original way. This can be really profitable because you will be the only person using the variable. For example, the American racing guru Andy Beyer made a fortune in the 1970s and early 1980s by assessing horses ability using speed figures because he had found a unique way of calculating them. Sectional time and pace analysis analysis might be a new frontier for systems players to conquer. The preferences of a sire on different types of going and distance are also areas of form study that are under researched in my view, as is the record of the major owners. These areas might be ones to look at when starting to develop a system as you are more likely to uncover a new nugget of information from the data.

Objective variables

When developing systems you should only use quantitative variables. In other words only use factors that can be measured in a consistent and objective manner. Avoid at all costs systems that rely on qualitative information. I know of many systems that use qualitative data on horse's looks. This is based on sound racing logic in that good looking horses are usually the most able because they have a good physique, and a high level of fitness. The problem is that what one-person judges too be a good looking horse another person will disagree. As an example I remember reading in Pat Taaffee's excellent autobiography *'My Life and Arkles'* a story about Lord Bicester who always purchased what he considered to be very good looking horses. When his horse Royal Approach won the Irish Grand National a former leading jockey patted the Lord on the back to congratulate him and said 'Good horse, but not much of a looker is he?" to which the Lord replied "when was the last time you looked in the mirror"! It is therefore better to steer clear of opinion and focus only on those variables that you can measure objectively. This means using only hard numerical data from than a subjective assessment.

Look for consistent profits

A number of so-called profitable systems do not record consistent levels of profit, year in, and year out. They often record a lucky year in which they make an extraordinary profit, which disguises the fact that in a normal year the system makes a loss. When testing systems it is therefore important to break down the results by year and note the level of profit recorded in each year. I am always much more confident of a system that has shown a consistent profit over time. I'm particularly interested in whether the system shows a profit across years in its validation sample. If you find a system that shows a consistent profit in its validation then get your betting boots on. One caveat here is to check to see whether the profitability of your system is the result of outliers e.g. one or two selections winning at extreme odds. The presence of these outliers might make a losing system look like a winning one. A consistently good record over a number of years might give you confidence that the system isn't relying just on long-priced winners.

However, you might not have enough years of data to be able to test this, especially in your validation sample. Furthermore systems that show a profit year-on-year are very rare. The great Dr Peter May, formerly of Raceform fame, once explained a good way of checking the reliability of a system by ordering all the winners according to their odds (highest to lowest) and then checking to see if the system was still profitable after deleting each long priced winner. The further down the list you got before the system broke even or would have made a loss would therefore give you an indication about whether the system was relying on a few long priced winners or was still profitable after several of these were removed.

You need to exercise a bit of judgement here because your system might be designed around picking long-priced winners, and therefore you need to work out what counts as an extreme long priced winner in this context. A good way to do this would be to calculate the mean and median price of all the winners in your systems sample of results. When you do this and you might notice that the mean price of the winners is much higher than the median price (e.g. the mean value is double the median value). This would be a warning signal that the profitability of your system might be biased by one or two extreme long-shot winners that win at a price far in excess of the typical winner for the system. For example your system might record most of its winners around the 10-1 price mark, but when you look at your data you see that the mean price of the winners is 20-1 because it had one winner at 100-1, which pushed up the mean value. The median price of all winners would therefore be closer to 10-1 as that statistical measure isn't influenced by the extreme value. In this case I'd knock out the 100-1 winner from my analysis and then see if the system was still profitable, but leave in all the winners priced at less than this. It is only the obvious outliers that you want to knock out because if you knock out too many long-priced winners from a strategy that is based around long-shots then you might overlook a genuinely profitable system.

Statistical significance

There are a number of statistical tests that you can use to test whether the results of your system are the result of chance or identifying genuine differences between winners and losers, and profits and losses. The details behind those tests are beyond the scope of this book but statistical tests such as the chi-square test and the t-test are two methods that you can use to measure statistical significance. These tests can be run in any statistical software package but are also available in Excel and other spreadsheet software. One thing to note is that when testing for statistical significance you should make sure that you are seeing statistically significant differences in both the development sample and in the validation sample that you are using to test the system against.

In this Chapter I have tried to offer a few pointers to developing betting systems. For those of you that like to try your hand at systems development I hope they prove useful and profitable.

CONCLUSION

Over the past decade the turnover from off-course horse race betting in the UK has significantly decreased from £5.7 billion in 2009 to £4.2 billion in 2019. Furthermore, while around £14 billion was gambled in the UK in 2019 the share accounted for by horse racing was down on the previous year, and this continues a downward. This is largely due to the increase seen in gambling on other sports, but also online bingo and casino games that have enjoyed a boom over the last few years. This is all very depressing for passionate racing fans like me and you. Horse racing is a game of skill whereas fixed odds betting terminals, and online roulette games, are games of chance and the odds are most definitely stacked against the punter.

The fact that horse racing is seeing a smaller share of the gambling pound means that there is more competition between punters to make a profit from the racing game, and to take their share of a dwindling pot. This trend is likely to continue and profitable punters are going to have to continually improve to stay ahead. This means that the modern winning punter is going to have to get smarter and more sophisticated in the way that they play the game.

The profitable punter in the twenty-first century will need to use bigger form databases; conduct more and more original research; develop new statistics that give them an edge; and embrace new tools that help them to do this. This is an ongoing battle.

In this book I've tried to present to you some of the research that I have done in recent years to help me stay ahead. However, this is really only to get you thinking. The edge from my systems and strategies will be quickly eroded, because other people will independently uncover them too, and the information will eventually get incorporated into the betting odds. My advice would be to keep your winning systems to yourself. I seem to have a psychological need to share my research with others. Certainly writing this book probably won't help maintain the shelf-life of my systems, but I expect that I am sharing them with a select audience!

In the months and years ahead I'll need to keep developing new ideas and will need to develop new systems and strategies to keep ahead of the crowd. I'm sure that you have got your own ideas about how you can take your share of the punting pound. Maybe you are also thinking about how you can upskill yourself to embrace the modern computer age; maybe you are thinking about how you can use the new forms of data that are slowly emerging on sectional times, and thinking of new ways to analyse a race; maybe you are working out some new systems and strategies, and thinking about how to automate them and use a bot program to place your bets.

The rest of the twenty-first century will be a challenging time for the winning punter, but it will also be rich in opportunities as new forms of data emerge and new software and technology become available to help the punter to better analyse the form book.

The racing game is always evolving. The profitable punter will always be the one that adapts the best to this ever changing environment. I hope that this book has given you some ideas that will help you stay ahead of the crowd. Good luck!

P.S.

I'd be interested to know how you get on, and for my part I will continue to share my latest research and analysis on profitablebetting.co.uk. You can keep me posted on your efforts via the same website. Could I also ask a favour? I hesitate to ask but if you have found this book to be of any interest then please feel free to give it a plug on Amazon. Best wishes.

Printed in Great Britain
by Amazon

83690311R00180